Dealing with Deindustrialization

The late 1970s and 1980s saw a process of mass factory closures in cities and regions across the Midwest of the United States. What happened next as leaders reacted to the news of each plant closure and to the broader deindustrialization trend that emerged during this time period is the main subject of this book.

It shows how leaders in eight metropolitan areas facing deindustrialization strived for adaptive resilience by using economic development policy. The unique attributes of each region – asset bases, modes of governance, civic capacity, leadership qualities, and external factors – influenced the responses employed and the outcomes achieved. Using adaptive resilience as a lens, Margaret Cowell provides a thorough understanding of how and why regions varied in their abilities to respond to deindustrialization.

Margaret Cowell, Assistant Professor of Urban Affairs and Planning, Virginia Tech.

Routledge Research in Planning and Urban Design

Series editor: Peter Ache

Radboud University Nijmegen, the Netherlands

Routledge Research in Planning and Urban Design is a series of academic monographs for scholars working in these disciplines and the overlaps between them. Building on Routledge's history of academic rigour and cutting-edge research, the series contributes to the rapidly expanding literature in all areas of planning and urban design.

Brand-Driven City Building and the Virtualizing of Space
Alexander Gutzmer

The Empty Place
Democracy and public space
Teresa Hoskyns

Deconstructing Placemaking
Mahyar Arefi

Public Space and Relational Perspectives
New challenges for architecture and planning
Chiara Tornaghi and Sabine Knierbein

Dealing with Deindustrialization
Adaptive resilience in american midwestern regions
Margaret Cowell

Dealing with Deindustrialization

Adaptive resilience in american midwestern regions

Margaret Cowell

Routledge
Taylor & Francis Group
LONDON AND NEW YORK

First published 2015 by Routledge

2 Park Square, Milton Park, Abingdon, Oxfordshire OX14 4RN
52 Vanderbilt Avenue, New York, NY 10017

Routledge is an imprint of the Taylor & Francis Group, an informa business

First issued in paperback 2020

British Library Cataloguing-in-Publication Data
A catalogue record for this book is available from the British Library

Library of Congress Cataloging-in-Publication Data
Cowell, Margaret.
Dealing with deindustrialization: adaptive resilience in American Midwestern regions/Margaret Cowell.
pages cm.—(Routledge research in planning and urban design)
Includes bibliographical references and index.
1. Economic development—Middle West. 2. Deindustrialization—Middle West. 3. Middle West—Economic conditions.
4. Middle West—Economic Policy. I. Title.
HC107.A14C69 2014
338.0977—dc23
2014013867

ISBN: 978-1-1387-9136-7 (hbk)
ISBN: 978-0-367-66925-6 (pbk)

Typeset in Sabon
by Swales and Willis Ltd, Exeter, Devon, UK

Dedication

To David and Mary-Jane Cowell
and to Joseph Murray

Contents

Figures

Tables

Preface

My interest in regional responses to economic challenges began long before this particular body of research commenced. Although I might not have always known it, I have been thinking about places and economies for decades. I spent most of my childhood in a very small city in Upstate New York. If you have heard of Oswego, NY, it is probably only because of its record snowfall or maybe because of the small college that is located there, the State University of New York (SUNY) at Oswego. The city is less well known for its main economic driver, a two-unit nuclear power plant called Nine Mile Point Nuclear Station. In 2006, when both units were being considered for re-licensing, there was great uncertainty amongst Oswegonians; local newspapers covered the re-licensing extensively and discussions surrounding this uncertainty were a main topic of conversation at many a retiree coffee klatch. Twenty-year license extensions were ultimately granted to both units and discussions then turned to whether or not a third unit would gain approval. Though that third unit would ultimately not be approved, the fate of the city and the surrounding economy, which have suffered greatly during recent economic downturns, now rests in the continued success of the two original power plants. Oswegonians have long known that jobs, taxes, and housing prices are all intertwined with the fate of the nuclear plants. Just like the Rust Belt leaders interviewed for this study, leaders in Oswego also find it difficult to ignore the possibility that the local economy will suffer greatly if the economic base is compromised.

While the challenges I observed in Oswego remain largely in the present or very near future, the difficulties discussed in this study unfolded many years ago. Nevertheless, my experiences in Oswego, and later on as an economist at the Buffalo Branch of the Federal Reserve Bank of New York, seem oddly reminiscent of the historical tensions I encountered in this research project. Rather than looking forward, this body of research looks back in history to examine industrial Midwestern metropolitan regions as they struggled with deindustrialization, which began to unravel regional economies during the late 1970s and early 1980s.

Though the broader goal of this research has always been to make relevant and increase our understanding of why some regions perform better than others in the wake of a crisis, I had little idea just how applicable this historical analysis would become. When I began this research in late 2007, the United States economy was performing relatively well and many regions across the country were reaping the benefits of that solid performance. A short while later, particularly in the fall of 2008, metropolitan areas began to struggle as our national economy experienced a marked deceleration of economic activity. Suddenly, the difficulty that places like Detroit and Pittsburgh experienced in the 1970s and 1980s became relevant again as other regions began to grapple with their own problems of widespread unemployment, paralyzing foreclosures, and general economic and fiscal instability. Though this recession and its aftermath did not play out in exactly the same way as those that occurred in the early 1980s, there are still many valuable lessons to be learned about how regions responded to these same challenges nearly three decades ago.

The book that follows is based on the idea that talking with decision makers of the past is one of the best ways to learn about successes and failures. In all, 96 individuals provided in-depth interviews. Though they were promised anonymity in exchange for their honest assessment of how things played out in their respective regions, I sincerely hope that their voices, in addition to mine, shine through in this historical narrative. I thank them for their anonymous contributions and am honored to have their participation in this important work. Any mistakes or misrepresentations are my own.

This research would not have been possible without the support (financial and otherwise) of numerous organizations. Thank you to the National Association of Counties for their generous financial backing during the dissertation fieldwork and to Virginia Tech's Institute for Society, Culture, and Environment for their support in the writing stage. Thanks also to all of the wonderful scholars I have met as a member of the MacArthur Foundation's research network on Building Resilient Regions. The fantastic research and professional guidance provided by network members and the financial support provided by the MacArthur Foundation were immensely helpful to me as I conducted this research.

Special mention must go to Nicole Solano, Editor at Routledge, who helped me navigate the complex publication process and helped me to refine my thinking and tighten the narrative. Moreover, I appreciate the assistance of Alex Hollingsworth, Senior Publisher, and Sadé Lee, Editorial Assistant, both of whom have been patient and immensely helpful in their attention to detail.

Thanks are also due to the faculty and staff in the Department of City and Regional Planning at Cornell University and the School of Public and International Affairs at Virginia Tech for their generous financial and administrative support throughout this process. The final steps of this process have been made much easier with support from my colleagues in the Urban Affairs and Planning Program at Virginia Tech, including Ralph Buehler, Derek Hyra, Shelley Mastran, Shallini Misra, Elizabeth Morton, John Provo,

Joseph Schilling, and Kris Wernstedt. Alanna McKeeman and Kelly Davis, graduate research assistants at Virginia Tech, provided endless assistance in the preparation of this manuscript, which made the whole process a lot more enjoyable. Thanks to them and the many other students who have inspired me both in the classroom and outside of it.

I am grateful for the encouragement of the professors who have forever influenced my research and my teaching. First, special thanks to Rolf Pendall, who gave me the courage to research and write about otherwise forgotten places. Thanks are also due to Susan Christopherson and Kieran Donaghy, two prolific scholars and mentors whose work has greatly inspired me and will undoubtedly continue to do so in the future. Thanks also to Kathryn Foster, a wonderful scholar, mentor, and friend.

Throughout this process I have been most fortunate to have the endless support of my family and many friends. For that, I am eternally grateful. First and foremost, I would like to thank my husband, Joseph Murray; my parents, David and Mary-Jane Cowell; my grandmother, Tiz; my sister, Molly; and my brother, David. Your support, encouragement, and patience (even across continents) have been invaluable to me, both now and forever. I also want to thank my good friend and colleague, Sara O'Neill-Kohl, for her incredible advice, encouragement, style, and grace. Thanks to Elizabeth Switzer for her artistic vision. And to Adam, Jenny, and Valerie thanks so much for your friendship and good energies sent from both near and far.

Introduction

On a Monday afternoon in September of 1983, Indianapolis Mayor William H. Hudnut III received a phone call from an executive at Western Electric. The executive announced that the company would close its Shadeland factory where nearly 8,000 people were employed making Princess telephones. This phone call, and the actions taken in its wake, affected the lives of thousands of people in Indianapolis, changed the course of economic development within the region, and forever altered the landscape of the regional economy. For Indianapolis, this call was a bellwether, sounding the deindustrialization alarm and signifying that this call might be one of many similar phone calls. But Indianapolis was not alone; mayors across the Midwest received the same kind of phone calls during the late 1970s and 1980s, signaling the closure, downsizing, or offshoring of their own hometown factories.

What happened next in each of these regions, as leaders reacted to the news of each plant closure and to the broader economic restructuring trend that emerged during this time period, is the main subject of this book. In it I uncover how leaders in eight metropolitan areas facing deindustrialization strived for adaptive resilience by using economic development policy. As part of this inquiry into adaptive resilience, I investigate how the unique attributes of each region – including regional asset bases, modes of governance, civic capacity, leadership qualities, and external factors – influenced the type of response employed and the outcomes achieved.

Despite the increasing interest in resilience studies, there is no single agreed-upon definition of adaptive resilience, especially in the face of persistent challenges like deindustrialization. Using adaptive resilience as a lens, I apply established theory and methods from this burgeoning body of literature to provide a more thorough understanding of how and why regions varied in their abilities to respond to deindustrialization. The analysis specifically focuses on the economic development responses in eight major Midwestern metropolitan regions: Buffalo, Cincinnati, Cleveland, Columbus, Detroit, Indianapolis, Milwaukee, and Pittsburgh (Figure I.1).

Rather than looking forward, this body of research looks back in history to examine industrial Midwestern metropolitan regions as they struggled with the economic restructuring that began to unravel regional economies

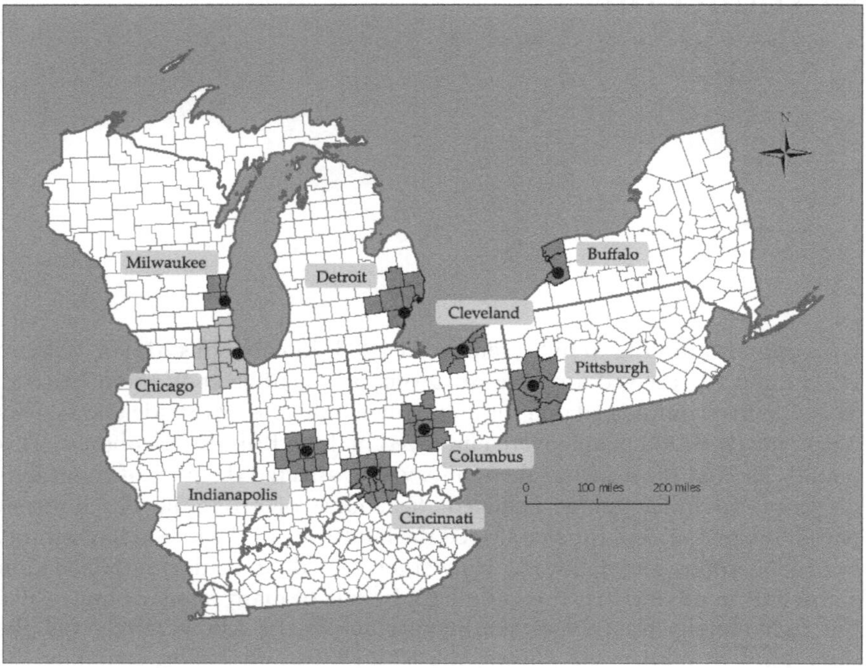

Figure I.1 The Rust Belt region with selected metropolitan regions
Source: Author.

during the late 1970s and early 1980s. Given the historically unprecedented nature of this economic challenge, decisions about how to respond were often quite difficult for regional leaders to make. In order to gain a diverse and robust understanding of each region's response, the book draws from current and historical economic and demographic data, archival data from planning and other public documents, and qualitative data collected through extensive interviews with former stakeholders from the public, private, and non-profit sectors.

Though the broader goal of this research has always been to make relevant and increase our understanding of why some regions perform better than others in the wake of a crisis, I had little idea just how applicable this research would become. When I began working on this project in early 2008, the United States economy was performing relatively well and many regions across the country were reaping the benefits of that solid performance. A short while later, particularly in the fall of 2008, metropolitan areas began to struggle as the national economy experienced a marked deceleration of economic activity. Suddenly, the difficulties that places like Detroit and Pittsburgh experienced in the 1970s and 1980s became relevant again today as regions began to grapple with their own problems of widespread unemployment, paralyzing foreclosures, and general economic and fiscal instability. Though this recession did not play out in exactly the same way as those that occurred in the early 1980s, there are still many valuable lessons to be learned about how regions responded to these same challenges nearly three decades ago. To that end, this book offers three major contributions in the areas of resilience studies, economic development, and urban planning.

First, it is among the first research studies to arrive at a functional definition of adaptive resilience. I utilize existing literature from ecology, psychology, urban planning, and other fields to develop a comprehensive and reflective definition of adaptive resilience that will help guide planners, practitioners, policymakers, and other leaders at the local and regional levels. We learn from ecologists and engineers that there are two main types of resilience: *ecological resilience*, which describes instances in which some sort of disruption pushes a system from one equilibrium to another; and *engineering resilience,* which is when a system returns to its presumed steady state after a disruption. Most planners would agree, however, that neither of these traditional conceptualizations of resilience is appropriate in cases of long-term challenges like deindustrialization where regional actors are not looking to achieve (or maintain) a new equilibrium, nor are they looking to simply 'bounce back' to their pre-challenge state. Instead, I introduce the concept of adaptive resilience and the notion that regions are adaptive systems, in which resilience is not necessarily related to equilibrium, a return to 'normal,' or even to resilient outcomes; it is instead a "dynamic attribute associated with a process of continual development" (Pendall, et al 2010).

Second, the book identifies distinct patterns in how eight regions responded to deindustrialization and how their respective responses contributed to or detracted from adaptive resilience. Namely, I show that regions that focused on the retention and expansion of existing manufacturing firms were less likely to exhibit adaptive resilience than those that chose to focus their economic development efforts on the attraction and growth of a more diverse economic base. I also conclude that timing matters; the regions that responded swiftly were more likely to exhibit adaptive resilience, while those that hesitated in their responses generally were not.

Third, the book serves as an archive of decision making in times of duress. It thoroughly documents both the actors involved in and the process of crafting an economic development response in the face of a significant challenge. Of particular import was the identification of the key decision makers involved in each case, along with a more thorough understanding of how these decision makers retrieved and processed information about their regional economy.

These eight regions have been selected because of their size: with the exception of Chicago, they were the only Rust Belt regions with populations greater than 1 million in 1980. Because of its extremely large size and the complexity of its response to deindustrialization, the Chicago region has been excluded from this study. The remaining eight regions vary significantly in terms of demographic composition, political leanings, and present-day economic bases; however, all are located within the Rust Belt, have storied manufacturing-intensive pasts, and have weathered significant challenges during the late-twentieth century.

This research builds upon previous case studies of economic development responses in Flint (Lord and Price 1992), Pittsburgh (Detrick 1999), Cleveland (Hill 1995), Youngstown (Safford 2004), and Buffalo (Foster 2006). These individual case study analyses provide valuable insight into how individual regions responded to economic change during the latter half of the twentieth century. However, one of the main drawbacks of the single case study approach is the inability to compare responses across cases. In the Rust Belt, such broad comparisons are helpful in determining commonalities and differences in terms of both the types of responses seen and the efficacy of these responses across regions. Somewhere between the wide breadth and shallow depth of a large-N analysis and the narrow breadth and profound depth of a single case study lies the small-N analysis utilized in this study (Chapters 5 and 6). Such an approach allows for a comparison across a select number of highly relevant cases and the subsequent development of conclusions related to these findings. In other words, the small-N study allows us "to develop 'thick' (complex or multidimensional) concepts and theories that are well-suited for description and for making inferences about simple causation on a small scale or in a few cases" (Coppedge 1999, 465). Drawing upon interviews with local stakeholders, this small-N study affords a broad yet thorough comparison of eight cases, all the while compromising little in the way of depth.

Much of the qualitative data collected for this study come from individual interviews with regional leaders from the 1970s and 1980s. Interviewees represent a cross-section of interests, jurisdictions, and sectors in each of the case study regions. Interviews in each region generally targeted stakeholders from the public, private, and civic sectors. Confidentiality was maintained because of the need to establish trust between the interviewees and myself and in order to promote the interviewees' autonomy and freedom to reflect honestly on wins and losses of the past. Additional archival research was also used to verify interviewees' answers.

This variety of perspectives allows for a more nuanced understanding of each region's situation during this particular moment in time. The quantitative data about national economic trends discussed in Chapters 2 and 4 come from the federal government, including the U.S. Census Bureau, Bureau of Economic Analysis, and Bureau of Labor Statistics. The qualitative data presented in Chapters 5 and 6, however, are primary data collected by the author through participant interviews for the purposes of this study. Other data come from local periodicals, planning documents, as well as state and local budgets.

In order to gain first-person accounts of the local decision-making process in these regions, 96 interviews with regional leaders were conducted between

2008 and 2011. The lists of stakeholders were culled from historical public records of relevant local, state, and regional meetings; previously published research on this time period; and by recommendation from other living stakeholders in the region. In most cases, initial contact was made with the staff of each region's current economic development agency. Current staff members were asked to identify the person who could best speak to the economic development decision-making process at the onset of deindustrialization. In most cases, I was referred to a former head of the local or regional economic development organization or government planning department. From there, I sought the names of stakeholders from the central city, surrounding counties, the major suburbs, and any related regional entities in existence. Attempts were then made to interview at least ten people from this list of stakeholders in each region. In all eight regions, participants reflected a diverse sample of interests, including leaders from both the private and public sectors and from offices with urban, suburban, and regional interests. Interviews specifically targeted the important players who made decisions about economic development planning and policy during the late 1970s and early 1980s.

Participants were asked about their perception of their region's economy during this time period, their responses to the economic changes that they saw unfolding, and their opinions on the efficacy of these responses. Interviewees were also asked to discuss the local effects of deindustrialization, the specific types of policies and programs implemented to address these effects, and the effectiveness of the chosen economic development strategies used in each of the eight Rust Belt regions. The interviews lasted between 60 and 90 minutes each and followed a standard protocol intended to elicit open-ended responses. Interviews were conducted either in person or via telephone and were recorded, transcribed, and then summarized.

These interviews and subsequent archival research were motivated by three main questions that guided this research. All three pertain to economic development in Rust Belt regions, albeit in slightly different ways. Together, they encourage us to consider the unique features of metropolitan regions, particularly during one important period of history, and how decision makers affect regional outcomes, either on their own or in combination with other important factors. The research questions are intended to steer us towards a better understanding of regions, regional leadership, and the intersection of the two.

Research questions

Stemming from a desire to learn more about the decisions being made in the wake of deindustrialization, I start by asking a seemingly simple question: *who was involved in crafting each region's economic development response to deindustrialization and how did they go about crafting it?* In the first part of this question, the overarching goal is to identify the main stakeholders involved in each region's decision-making process. Then, once these leaders have been identified, I seek to understand the decision-making process itself in each of the eight case study regions. Identifying the people who are sitting at the 'decision-making table' goes a long way in explaining a region's power dynamic. For instance, in a region ruled largely by the economic elite the response plan might be geared towards policies and practices that will aid their own firm or their own economic sector. Or, in a region where political leadership is strong, the recovery plan might be geared towards workforce development and various other constituent-friendly types of strategies. Therefore, knowing who is at the table is helpful information in that it focuses in on potential interviewees who help us to both better understand their region's decision-making process and gain insight into the types of actors involved in this process.

Building on the findings from this first question, the second research question urges us to consider the underlying rationale of each region's economic development response. Knowing who was 'at the table' gives us some general insight as to the kinds of issues that were likely discussed but tells us little about specific agendas. To gain a better understanding of what it is that regional leaders wanted from the economic development response, we must ask another question: *what were the specific motivations or goals of each region's economic development response?* Answering this question will then facilitate the mapping of each region's response against longer-term outcomes.

Once we know more about the primary players and their motivations, we can then begin thinking about how these components relate to adaptive resilience. More specifically, we can ask a third research question: *to what extent did these regions exhibit adaptive resilience as they confronted the challenges associated with deindustrialization?* In other words, findings from the first two research questions urge us to consider how well each region adapted and responded to the challenge of deindustrialization by way of economic development. In order to answer this question, we will discuss adaptive resilience and also uncover more detailed information about the particular strengths, weaknesses, assets, and liabilities of each case study region.

The motivation for all three research questions comes from the fact that the relationship between adaptive resilience and economic development is not clear and is likely different for each individual region. In order to better understand that relationship, it is necessary to weave together a more holistic understanding of how regions respond throughout the entire adaptive cycle. It would be imprudent to examine one simple aggregate indicator to determine resilience; instead, we must understand how the engagement of actors, the setting of an agenda, and, eventually, economic development interventions all determine whether or not a region has exhibited adaptive resilience in the face of a given challenge.

The following chapters help us to answer these and other questions. In Chapter 1, I introduce you to (or reacquaint you with) the United States Rust Belt, explore the concept of deindustrialization, and discuss typologies that have been useful in studying this trend. I show that variations in how deindustrialization played out at both the regional and sub-regional levels can be explained by a variety of factors including local and regional assets, history, leadership, governmental structure, and politics. Resilience is the focus of Chapter 2. In particular, I provide a brief overview of how resilience has been conceived in other fields and describe how it can be modified for useful application to regions experiencing longer-term challenges like deindustrialization and economic restructuring. I conclude with a definition of adaptive resilience to guide planners, practitioners, policymakers, and other leaders at the local and regional level. In Chapter 3, the focus is on the practice of economic development as a response to deindustrialization. I explain how Rust Belt regions simultaneously grappled with deindustrialization and a shift in the way that economic development was conceived, funded, and executed. The implications of this shift, including changes in the tools and funding streams available, are discussed in detail. The eight regions included in this research are briefly described in Chapter 4 along with fundamental analyses of each region's economic base, as well as their recent economic, social, and political histories. Initial hypotheses are also provided in Chapter 4.

The bulk of the case study findings are presented in Chapters 5 and 6. One of the more common regional responses to the challenges of deindustrialization was to struggle against change, ignore calls for diversification, and attempt to recreate the economic base of the past. Chapter 5 describes how four of the case study regions – Buffalo, Cleveland, Detroit, and Milwaukee – chose this approach, and shows how their 'Betting on the Basics' response ultimately detracted from adaptive resilience within their respective regions. Chapter 6 explores the approaches taken in the remaining regions: Cincinnati, Columbus, Indianapolis, and Pittsburgh. In these places regional leaders took steps to consciously move beyond what was easiest or what was familiar in hopes of reaching a better long-term outcome. By 'Bowing Out,' these regions actively or flexibly turned the corner away from basic manufacturing and fared comparatively well by most measures of adaptive resilience. Both Chapters 5 and 6 conclude by comparing regional outcomes and by presenting lessons we might take away from the two main types of economic development responses observed in these places.

Final conclusions about the resilience of regions in the face of deindustrialization are presented in Chapter 7. In order to do this, I first revisit, and then discuss, the three hypotheses presented in Chapter 4. I then propose a series of remaining questions about the benefits of certain economic development response types, the preconditions necessary for certain responses, and the usefulness of adaptive resilience as a framing concept for studies of regional economic development. The book concludes with a discussion of how we might consider these findings in light of the more recent Great Recession.

Limitations

It should be noted that in this project, as is the case in all research projects, there are some limitations. First and foremost, focusing specifically on the Rust Belt limits the generalizability of the research findings to some extent. Although the focused nature of the subset analyses will allow for a multi-faceted approach to studying economic development responses to deindustrialization, this study will not be generalizable to all types of deindustrializing regions. In particular, other regions, especially in other countries, may face their own unique constraints because of differences in local, external, civic, and other pressures. A basic scan of the literature suggests that other areas of the world have experienced deindustrialization in different ways and at different times than we saw in the United States Rust Belt during the 1970s and 1980s (Rowthorn and Ramaswamy 1997; DiGaetano and Lawless 1999). Even within the United States, deindustrialization has occurred in different ways and at different times (see Koistinen 2000 on New England and Minchin 2009 on North Carolina).

Furthermore, divergent outcomes also exist within regions at the sub-regional scale. Because there rarely are responses developed that are truly regional in nature, it is sometimes necessary to study a variety of sub-regional responses in order to get a sense of how the region responded as a whole. Researchers have come to believe that the strength of a given region depends, at least in part, on the strength of the region's central city or cities (Ihlanfeldt 1994; Voith 1996). When you strive to learn about regional success based on sub-regional strategies, the findings are inherently less generalizable and less conclusive. Though these place-specific conclusions may ultimately limit the generalizability of this research, the lessons we learn from these regions of the Rust Belt will likely outweigh any limits we experience in terms of generalizability. Because it is the metropolitan scale that we are most concerned with, most findings will pertain to a given metropolitan region as a whole. In more complex cases where there are stark contrasts between a city and the region in which it is located, I make every effort to differentiate between the various parts.

Second, the research is somewhat limited in that it is impossible to definitively determine cause and effect, especially in historical cases like those explored in this study. In other words, it is difficult to determine whether specific interventions caused the outcomes observed in these regions or whether those outcomes would have been observed without any intervention. Researchers have noted the difficulty in determining the efficacy of local and regional economic development programs and policies in general (Pressman and Wildavsky 1984), and specifically in the face of highly mobile capital and a national policy supporting trade liberalization (Schumpeter 1982; Demetriades and Hussein 1996). In so doing, their findings encourage us to document past interventions as a way of continuing our exploration of the relationship between economic development interventions and outcomes. Documentation of these historical interventions will bring us one step closer to understanding how economic development responses shape regional outcomes.

Because so much time has passed since many of these events took place, some of the interviewees may have had difficulty correctly remembering the specific details of certain recollections. As such, some of the qualitative data run the risk of being historically inaccurate or imprecise. In all eight regions, additional efforts were made to cross-reference events and recollections to verify their accuracy. In most cases this was done through the examination of economic development plans and other archival documents from the 1970s and 1980s. In some cases, follow-up interviews were also conducted to confirm the veracity and timing of certain historically significant events.

In the end, this research represents one researcher's honest attempt to answer fundamental questions about regional responses to deindustrialization. Despite these potential limitations, the information presented in this book will likely be of use to regions (and their leaders) confronting slow-burning challenges like deindustrialization in the future. Overall, the research shows how regions confronting deindustrialization varied both in their responses and in their outcomes and illustrates how some regions successfully navigated this difficult time period while others are still fighting to reverse or curtail its negative effects. Like any good research project, this work answers a few questions and raises many more. I take comfort in the fact that we still have more to learn about regions, economic development, and resilience, and hope to further engage in research that answers these remaining questions. Until then, let this body of research serve as a reminder of all that we knew, all that we now know, and all that remains to be uncovered at the intersection of adaptive resilience, economic development, and deindustrialization.

References

Coppedge, Michael. 1999. "Thickening Thin Concepts and Theories: Combining Large N and Small in Comparative Politics." *Comparative Politics* 31(4): 465–476.

Demetriades, Panicos, and Khaled Hussein. 1996. "Does Financial Development Cause Economic Growth? Time-series Evidence from 16 Countries." *Journal of Development Economics* 51(2): 387–411.

Detrick, Sabina. 1999. "The Post Industrial Revitalization of Pittsburgh: Myths and Evidence." *Journal of Planning Literature* 34(1): 4–12.

DiGaetano, Joe, and Paul Lawless. 1999. "Urban Governance and Industrial Decline: Governing Structures and Policy Agendas in Birmingham and Sheffield, England, and Detroit, Michigan, 1980–1997." *Urban Affairs Review* 34(4): 546–577.

Foster, Kathryn. 2006. "A Case Study Approach to Understanding Regional Resilience." Working Paper 2007–08. University of California (November).

Hill, Edward. 1995. "The Cleveland Economy: A Case Study of Economic Restructuring." In *Cleveland: A Metropolitan Reader*, edited by W. Dennis Keating, Norman Krumholz, and David C. Perry, 53–86. Kent, OH: The Kent State University Press.

Ihlanfeldt, Keith. 1994. "The Importance of the Central City to the Regional and National Economy: A Review of the Arguments and Empirical Evidence," Policy Research Center, Georgia State University.

Koistinen, David. 2000. "Dealing with Deindustrialization: Economics, Politics, and Policy during the Decline of the New England Textile Industry, 1920–1960." *Unpublished dissertation*. Yale University.

Lord, George F., and Albert C. Price. 1992. "Growth Ideology in a Period of Decline: Deindustrialization and Restructuring, Flint Style." *Social Problems* 39(2): 155–169.

Minchin, Timothy. 2009. "'It Knocked This City to its Knees': The Closure of Pillowtex Mills in Kannapolis, North Carolina and the Decline of the US Textile Industry." *Labor History* 50(3): 287–311.

Pendall, Rolf, Kathryn Foster, and Margaret Cowell. 2010. "Resilience and Regions: Building Understanding of the Metaphor." *Cambridge Journal of Regions, Economy and Society* 3(1): 71–84.

Pressman, Jeffrey and Aaron Wildavsky. 1984. *Implementation: How Great Expectations in Washington are Dashed in Oakland*. Berkeley, CA: University of California Press.

Rowthorn, Robert, and Ramana Ramaswamy. 1997. "Deindustrialization: Causes and Implications." In *Staff Studies for the World Economic Outlook*, edited by International Monetary Fund, 61–77. Washington, DC: IMF.

Safford, Sean. 2009. *Why the Garden Club Couldn't Save Youngstown: The Transformation of the Rust Belt*. Cambridge, MA: Harward University Press.

Schumpeter, Joseph. 1982. *The Theory of Economic Development*. Cambridge, MA: Harvard University Press.

Voith, Richard P. 1996. "Central City Decline: Regional or Neighborhood Solutions?" *Federal Reserve Bank of Philadelphia Business Review* (March/April).

1 Deindustrialization and its discontents

Over the course of the early-to mid-twentieth century, millions of people, including many African-Americans coming from the south, migrated to cities like Detroit, Pittsburgh, and Indianapolis (Wilkerson 2010). Stable employment, union protection, and the potential for middle-class advancement drew workers and employers alike. Most employment opportunities for new arrivals and existing residents were in factories that produced steel, iron, or other related products. Tremendous gains in these industries tracked closely with the economic and population growth seen in the cities in which they were concentrated. Significant gains during the 1960s meant that the average US family took home one-third more real spendable income in 1970 than it did in 1960 (Bluestone 2003, viii). Within the Midwest, these gains were even more pronounced as manufacturers gained ground on foreign competition during the 1960s and 1970s.

All that would begin to change in the late 1970s and early 1980s, when metropolitan areas in the Midwest began to struggle with a precipitous loss of jobs and widespread outmigration to other parts of the country and the world. These changes often coincided with a shift in economic bases from manufacturing-intensive to more services-based economies. Such a transition was difficult for most Midwestern regions because it generally meant simultaneously confronting population outmigration, above average unemployment, and diminished revenue. Further difficulty stemmed from dwindling and often uncertain federal support for the very economic development initiatives that would ostensibly make this transition easier. In order to understand how and why regional responses to these challenges were developed, we must first understand the unique characteristics of this region and the challenges it faced at the end of the twentieth century. We begin first with an exploration of the Rust Belt and its introduction to the popular imagination.

The United States Rust Belt

During the early- to mid-twentieth century the industrial Midwest was known for its manufacturing prowess, higher than average wages, and plentiful employment opportunities. Within the Midwest, steel and iron production, automobile manufacturing and related supporting industries, mainly component parts and assembly, were the primary economic drivers. This strong manufacturing base brought prosperity, stability, and opportunity for metropolitan regions in the Midwest during the 1950s, 1960s, and 1970s. At its peak during the 1970s, manufacturing accounted for one-fifth to one-third of nonfarm employment in states like Michigan, Indiana, Ohio, and Wisconsin (Rosen 1984).

Today, in stark contrast, many of these same regions conjure up images of rusted machinery, padlocked gates, and abandoned industrial compounds (Safford 2009). Much of this change occurred during the 1970s and 1980s through widespread economic restructuring – often called deindustrialization – that would alter the face of regional economies the world over. Metropolitan areas of the industrial Midwest experienced devastating losses in the form of disappearing jobs, population outmigration, and dwindling tax revenue. As a whole, the region saw 23.6 percent of its manufacturing employment disappear during this time period (Kahn 1997), which is one of the main reasons that the term hollowing out is used to describe this era (Safford 2009).

The idea of a Rust Belt first emerged in 1984 when Democratic presidential candidate Walter Mondale accused President Ronald Reagan of turning the Midwest into a "Rust Bowl." Accounts from that time period show that the press then popularized the term Rust Belt as a way to describe the Midwest and the decline that defined it. Over time, use of the term grew substantially, so that the term Rust Belt eventually became synonymous with a group of former steel- and auto-manufacturing metropolitan areas in an indefinite state of decline.

The United States Rust Belt has imprecise boundaries, but is generally thought to include the industrialized portions of the states that make up the Great Lakes region. When most people refer to the Rust Belt, they often include the entire states of Michigan and Ohio, northern and central Indiana, northern Illinois, southern Wisconsin, and the western portions of Pennsylvania and New York. These boundaries encompass the eight metropolitan areas included in this study.

The term Rust Belt emerged as a symbolic counterpoint to the Sunbelt – the more prosperous southern and southwestern area of the United States that stretches from Florida and Georgia to the southern portion of California. The Sunbelt, which also has imprecise boundaries, generally represented the more hopeful side of the industrial restructuring equation. For profit-driven companies, the south and southwest offered lower wages, immigrant labor, and the growing demand of retirement communities. For job seekers, the Sunbelt offered opportunities for employment in innovative technologies, oil extraction, and defense, as well as less expensive housing. As the Rust Belt bled jobs and people during the 1980s and 1990s, the Sunbelt saw exponential growth in population, housing, and employment.

More recently, the concept of a Rust Belt has gained ground in other parts of the world. European scholars and practitioners alternatively refer to their declining regions as part of a European Rust Belt or as an amalgamation of

Shrinking Cities (Hospers 2004). Both refer to very similar trends at play in places like Northern England and the Ruhr Area of Germany (Kühn and Liebmann 2007). The Rust Belt term has also been applied to the northern Chinese provinces of Heilongjiang, Jilin, and Liaoning, which have similarly suffered precipitous decreases in manufacturing output and employment (Li 2004).

Deindustrialization

One of the main identifying features of the Rust Belt region is the pronounced losses that most of its metropolitan areas saw during deindustrialization, which is in and of itself a contentious term. Deindustrialization as an idea was made popular in 1982 when Bluestone and Harrison released their benchmark study, *The Deindustrialization of America*, but the trend was underway long beforehand. Following sustained employment growth during much of the 1970s, the three-year period between 1979 and 1982 saw employment at the national scale grind to a startling halt (Rosen 1984). In particular, two downturns during this period had profoundly negative effects on heavy manufacturing, like automobiles, steel, tires, and machinery. The first downturn, the 1979 energy crisis that followed the 1979 Islamic Revolution in Iran, exacerbated US energy woes already reeling from the earlier 1973 crisis. The second quickly followed as a formal recession that lasted from July 1981 through November 1982 (NBER 2009). Together, these two downturns severely affected key industries in the Rust Belt and helped hasten the decline of many of its metropolitan areas.

In order to understand how deindustrialization affected the eight case study regions, it is useful to first recognize the origins and complexities of the deindustrialization trend. Part of the difficulty in understanding deindustrialization stems from the fact that the term is not often used by researchers today; in the United States, deindustrialization typically refers to the changes seen in the economy and in broader society during the late 1970s and early 1980s. The term is a historical construct, meaning that it happened during a certain point in history and was a construct of larger local and global economic processes, including trade liberalization and a growing spatial division of labor (Cowie and Heathcott 2003).

The term deindustrialization is also slightly confusing because it is a misnomer. Deindustrialization in the Rust Belt in no way resulted in *no industry*; instead, deindustrialization was part of a major economic restructuring that would change the economic landscape and industrial composition of these regions forever. In the United States, global restructuring of the manufacturing sector often meant that many corporate headquarters positions would stay put but lower-wage jobs were outsourced to less expensive areas of the world. In places like the Rust Belt, these higher-wage headquarter positions remained an important part of the regional economy but represented a comparatively smaller portion of total regional employment.

In most Rust Belt regions, deindustrialization caused a sharp downturn in low- and medium-wage manufacturing jobs and a gradual uptick in service sector employment. In other words, *industries* could still be found in these regions, just not in the same proportions or magnitudes as they had been in the past. Despite these losses in employment, improved efficiencies and mechanization actually increased output for some industries. However, the main focus in this book is on jobs and not output because economic development targets are most often tied to employment.

At its most basic level, deindustrialization is generally defined as the relative decline of the manufacturing sector (Bluestone and Harrison 1982). Providing an expansion of this fundamental definition, researchers have offered a variety of increasingly complex definitions with varying degrees of specialization. Kutscher and Personick (1986) describe deindustrialization as a lack of investment in basic production that, when combined with plant closings and layoffs, results in a large negative merchandise trade balance. A more relativist definition is provided by Pieper (1999), who defines the trend as a relative loss – with respect to the rest of the economy – of the industrial sector's contribution to overall labor productivity growth.[1]

Looking at deindustrialization as it pertains to actual places, the Federal Reserve Bank of New York released a report in the spring of 2006 on the state of manufacturing in the United States, primarily focusing on the upper Midwestern states, a region that is basically one and the same with the Rust Belt. Its research concluded that much of this area had seen widespread and persistent decline in the manufacturing sector from the 1980s forward. Though not all Rust Belt regions have been affected similarly, the analysts presented evidence that the United States overall has lost more than 5 million manufacturing jobs in the last three decades and that the share of the US labor force employed in this sector has dropped from 20 percent in 1979 to less than 11 percent in 2006 (Deitz and Orr 2006). The authors predict that these losses – many of which stem from a shedding of lower-skilled workers in a move towards higher-skilled and less labor-intensive production – will likely continue in the long term and continue to plague the Rust Belt region.

That structural change has occurred in the Rust Belt is generally accepted by economists today; looking back, however, to the time when this trend first began to unfold, we see that such an assertion was not always accepted. During the early 1980s, economists grappled with the issue of whether changes in industrial composition could best be described as cyclical or structural in nature. In 1982, Robert Lawrence and his colleagues at Brookings Institution argued that most employment losses related to plant closings at that time were only cyclical in nature and not permanent. He was not alone in thinking that deindustrialization was a myth and that cyclical change, rather than structural change, better described the industrial shifts happening in the late 1970s and 1980s (Branson 1983).

Alternative views citing a more structural type of change were given by Thurow (1980), Bluestone and Harrison (1982), and Magaziner and Reich

(1983), among others. Thurow, who was the first to coin the term "sunrise industries", argued that structural changes in the economy had paralyzed government's ability to assist in economic recovery. He advocated for focused government investment in sunrise industries, including high technology production and service activities. Bluestone and Harrison (1982), who provided empirical evidence of structural change in the United States, argued that deindustrialization resulted from the increased mobility of capital and a systematic shift in resources to low-cost locations. Bluestone followed with a 1984 article, "Is Deindustrialization a Myth? Capital Mobility versus Absorptive Capacity in the U.S. Economy", which found that notable job losses transpired in many basic industries throughout the Midwest. Primarily in agreement with Bluestone and Harrison, Magaziner and Reich (1983) proposed a series of policies and plans to improve the relationship between industry and government as a way of combating the structural change seen as a result of deindustrialization. In the end, those who supported structural change seemingly won out, as it is commonly believed today that the industrial structure of regions within the Rust Belt underwent permanent and often irreversible changes as evidenced by the substantial permanent job losses seen in key basic industries (Varaiya and Wiseman 1981).

Within the structural change camp, further hypothesizing about the causes of deindustrialization also occurred. From this discourse emerged two main theories: the concept of post-industrial society seen through the lens of product cycle theory and the concept of capital mobility seen through the lens of industrial relations theory. Although both theories contribute to our understanding of deindustrialization, they differ widely in their discussion of global and local forces.

Product cycle theorists generally believe that long-term patterns of international trade are influenced by product innovation and subsequent diffusion. The product cycle theory draws upon Ricardo's (1821) model of comparative advantage, which posited that diffusion is the natural process whereby businesses move toward places where their inputs can be obtained less expensively. Thus, the international diffusion of manufacturing during the late 1970s and 1980s may have been inevitable, as it is a necessary component of the product life cycle. It makes sense, then, that in a post-industrial society the growth and decline of regions reflects the life cycle of its core industries as they move through the processes of maturation, decentralization, and ultimately relocation. Through the lens of product cycle theory, plant closings were seen as part of a natural transformation from manufacturing and production to service-based and administrative jobs (Yago et al. 1984).

Industrial organizational theory, on the other hand, explained plant closings as a consequence of increased capital mobility (Ibid.). Underlying this increase in capital mobility was a surge in North-South trade and fierce international competition. Lee (2005) argued that "Southern import penetration, accompanied by low-wage competitive advantage, has led rich Northern countries to withdraw from the traditional low-skill intensive manufacturing industries" (72). Similarly, Lee found that international competition often resulted in multinational firms searching for cheaper labor and less restrictive regulations of labor and environments abroad (73). Exacerbating this trend in the Rust Belt was the rise of large, multi-locational firms, which tend to be less accountable to the region in which they are located because of the relative ease with which production could be moved to lower-wage regions in the US and elsewhere.

Today, there is still little consensus about the cause of deindustrialization. However, evidence from both the product life cycle theorists and the industrial organization camp is important to keep in mind as we consider how economic developers and local leaders responded to deindustrialization. One can imagine how responses might be different in regions where leaders subscribed to product life cycle theory and Thurow's notion of "sunrise industries" versus the responses developed in regions where industrial organization theory and international competition were the primary concern. We return to this idea and the divergence that emerges when regions respond differently in Chapters 5 and 6.

Global forces with regional and local implications

When we distill the existing research on deindustrialization it becomes clear that there is still much to learn about its causes, its effects, and its implications for various regions. Knowing that deindustrialization was a very complicated and nuanced phenomenon, we can ascertain that it affected each case study region, and its subcomponents, in slightly different ways. For some regions, job losses were swift and devastating. For others, the losses were gradual but unrelenting. Still other places saw minimal job losses or central city losses that were masked by gains in other parts of the region. Such variations in how deindustrialization played out at both the regional and sub-regional levels can likely be explained by a variety of factors including local and regional assets, history, leadership, governmental structure, and politics (Hill et al. 2008).

While these differences will be addressed in subsequent chapters, it is important here, in the context of a deindustrialization discussion, to flesh out how different sectors of manufacturing were affected by deindustrialization at the global scale. Though an overview of the sectoral specializations in each case study region will not be provided until Chapter 4 (when a more thorough exploration is possible), a basic understanding of the Rust Belt tells us that within the manufacturing sector there were two main specialties for which most metropolitan regions were known: steel manufacturing and automobile production. Deindustrialization affected both industries substantially but in slightly different ways.

Between the onset of the industrial revolution and the end of World War II, steel production grew in proportion to an ever-increasing global demand, especially during wartime. As production capacity grew and demand began to wane during the post-war period, the global market became saturated and steel prices saw a steep and swift decline, particularly during the 1970s (Revenga 1992). The downturn was especially detrimental to the steel economies of the Rust Belt, causing production and employment to slow dramatically in the late 1970s and 1980s (Crandall 1996). Though some of this employment loss was due to improved technological efficiencies, much of it was due to outsourcing and disinvestment. Such losses affected steel-intensive regions immensely because steel jobs were generally union jobs with high wages and good benefits. If these jobs were replaced at all, it was often with lower-paying jobs in the service sector (Sassen 1990).

Like the steel industry, the automobile industry experienced rapid growth during World Wars I and II (Ingrassia and White 1995). In the automobile industry, however, that growth continued through the 1950s, with the exception of the Great Depression. During the 1940s and 1950s, automobile production – led by General Motors, Cadillac and Ford – became a symbol of American prosperity. However, beginning in the 1960s and 1970s, Asian and European automobile manufacturers began to enter the United States market, gradually capturing market share with their smaller, more reliable, and generally less expensive vehicles (Dohse et al. 1985). As foreign automobiles gained ground in the 1970s and 1980s, sales of American-made automobiles fell off gradually, causing massive devastation in many Rust Belt regions (High 2003). Additional employment losses in automobile manufacturing also occurred when manufacturers looked to mechanization as a way to lower production costs, improve efficiencies, and increase profits (Schoenberger 1987). In total, the United States saw a loss of approximately 500,000 motor vehicles and equipment jobs between 1979 and 1982, the majority of which were located in the United States Rust Belt (Singleton 1992).

Compounding these job losses in the auto industry were additional losses seen in related sectors like parts production, which were generally located in regions within the Rust Belt. As Bluestone and Harrison (1982) noted, "The biggest losers in this instance are those who work in closely allied industries such as steel, rubber, metalworking machinery, and metal stampings" (72). In other words, losses in automobile production jobs beget serious losses in many other related industries, including steel. Given that many of these related components were produced in other metropolitan areas, one can begin to grasp how interdependent these regions really were.

From the aforementioned literature, we can state confidently that deindustrialization occurred within the United States Rust Belt during the latter part of the twentieth century. We can also assert that it affected individual regions within the Rust Belt in different ways and at different times. From the sectoral analysis we learn that global economic forces affected each industry in different ways and at slightly different times. We return to this subject in Chapter 4, but for now we are left with the understanding that economic restructuring affected various sectors of the economy differently, varying by time and degree. For a researcher, such variation is simultaneously challenging and rewarding; it is challenging in that it causes difficulty in identifying research-worthy commonalities and rewarding because it affords us the opportunity to uncover interesting and potentially useful threads across cases.

A note on nomenclature and emerging scholarship

In recent years we have witnessed a growing debate about nomenclature (see Power et al. 2010 on 'phoenix cities,' Pallagst 2010 on 'shrinking cities,' and Schilling and Mallach 2012 on 'Cities in Transition'). Regardless of what they call these places, there has generally been tremendous growth in both academic and practitioner interest regarding best practices for cities grappling with decline, restructuring, or other forms of stress (Cooke 2003; Florida 2003; Schilling and Logan 2008; Pendall et al. 2010; Hollander 2011; Savitch 2011). Beyond the Rust Belt there is a growing body of scholarship investigating similarly challenged cities and regions across the world. *Legacy Cities* – a concept typically used to describe post-industrial cities in the United States and Western Europe – are cities dealing with the adverse effects of long-term outmigration, economic restructuring, and deindustrialization (Mallach 2012). Interest in Legacy Cities has grown in part because of increasing international interest among practitioners and scholars who want to learn how to deal effectively with the interrelated challenges of population outmigration and decline. Scholarship relating to 'Cities in Transition,' a broader term used to describe cities facing major challenges of regeneration resulting from fundamental short- or long-term changes, has also gained attention in recent years (Schilling and Mallach 2012).

A rapidly growing network is emerging amongst and between scholars in many United States and European cities. In 2004, the Shrinking Cities International Research Network (SCiRN) was founded in Germany, focusing on comparative research on shrinking cities globally. In the United States, a Shrinking Cities research group has coalesced within the University of California Berkeley's Center for Global Metropolitan Studies. Within these networks, a collection of case studies, historical analyses, policy design evaluations, and assessments of program interventions, including deconstruction, land banking, code enforcement, and innovative reuse approaches, has begun to take shape.

The growing national and international interest in Shrinking or Legacy Cities is important to Rust Belt regions and other regions grappling with the ill-effects of deindustrialization and outmigration. Though Rust Belt regions, Shrinking Cities, and Legacy Cities are a diverse lot, they share common problems and challenges and can learn much from one another. Comparative and collaborative research is essential to expanding the policy debate beyond the local level and connecting local leaders to state and national venues, where greater funding and legislative reach may provide more opportunity (Beauregard 2012). Establishing these relationships will be especially important for practitioners and policymakers as tax bases diminish and funding becomes increasingly scarce. Researchers can play a key role in identifying how, and at what scale, a policy or program is most likely to achieve positive outcomes. This is an important task, to which we will return later on in the book.

Note

1 Still other researchers recognize the interplay between demographic and economic shifts. Emphasizing the importance of shrinking populations in deindustrializing regions, Van der Gaag et al. (1999) define such a process as negative natural population growth as a result of declining fertility levels and increasing numbers of deaths due to aging. In their research on declining populations in the European Union, the researchers concluded that the sharpest population losses have been observed in economically less prosperous regions (Van der Gaag et al. 1999).

References

Beauregard, Robert. 2012. "Research on Shrinking Cities." In *Cities in Transition: A Guide for Practicing Planners*, by Joseph Schilling and Alan Mallach, 24–25. American Planning Association PAS Report. Chicago, IL: APA.

Bluestone, Barry. 1984. "Is Deindustrialization a Myth? Capital Mobility versus Absorptive Capacity in the U.S. Economy." *Annals of the American Academy of Political and Social Science* 475: 39–51.

Bluestone, Barry. 2003. "Foreword." In *Beyond the Ruins: The Meaning of Deindustrailization,* edited by Jefferson Cowie and Joseph Heathcott, vii–xiv. Ithaca, NY: ILR Press.

Bluestone, Barry, and Bennett Harrison. 1982. *The Deindustrialization of America.* New York: Basic Books.

Branson, William. 1983. "Myth of De-industrialization." *Regulation* 7(5): 24–29.

Cooke, Phillip. 2003. "Keeping the High Road: Learning, Reflexivity, and Associative Governance in Regional Economic Development." In *The Rise of the Rustbelt*, edited by Phillip Cooke, 231–246. London: Routledge.

Cowie, Jefferson, and Joseph Heathcott, eds. 2003. *Beyond the Ruins: The Meanings of Deindustrialization.* Ithaca, NY: Cornell University Press.

Crandall, Robert W. 1996. "From Competitiveness to Competition: The Threat of Minimills to Large National Steel Companies." *Resources Policy* 22(1): 107–118.

Deitz, Richard, and James Orr. 2006. "A Leaner, More Skilled U.S. Manufacturing Workforce." *Current Issues in Economics and Finance* 12(2): 1–7.

Dohse, Knuth, Ulrich Jurgens, and Thomas Nialsch. 1985. "From 'Fordism' to 'Toyotism'? The Social Organization of the Labor Process in the Japanese Automobile Industry." *Politics & Society* 14: 115–146.

Florida, Richard. 2003. "The Industrial Transformation of the Great Lakes Region." In *The Rise of the Rustbelt*, edited by Phillip Cooke, 231–246. London: Routledge.

High, Steven. 2003. *Industrial Sunset: The Making of North America's Rust Belt, 1969–1984*, Toronto: University of Toronto Press.

Hill, Edward, Howard Wial, and Harold Wolman. 2008. "Exploring Regional Economic Resilience." Washington, DC: The Brookings Institution.

Hollander, Justin. 2011. "Can a City Successfully Shrink? Evidence from Survey Data on Neighborhood Quality." *Urban Affairs Review* 47(1): 129–141.

Hospers, Gert-Jan. 2004. "Restructuring Europe's Rustbelt." *Intereconomics* 39(3): 147–156.

Ingrassia, Paul, and Joseph B. White. 1995. *Comeback: The Fall and Rise of the American Automobile Industry*. New York: Simon and Schuster.

Kahn, Matthew E. 1997. "The Silver Lining of Rust Belt Manufacturing Decline: Killing Off Pollution Externalities." Center for Economic Studies, Bureau of the Census, 1997.

Kühn, Manfred, and Heike Liebmann. 2007. "Strategies for Urban Regeneration – The Transformation of Cities in Northern England and Eastern Germany." In *Restructuring Eastern Germany*, edited by S. Lentz, 123–138. New York: Springer.

Kutscher, Ronald E., and Valerie A. Personick. 1986. "Deindustrialization and the Shift to Services." *Monthly Labor Review* (June): 3–13.

Lee, Cheol-Sung. 2005. *International Migration, Deindustrialization and Union Decline in 16 Affluent OECD countries, 1962–1997*. Chapel Hill, NC: University of North Carolina Press.

Li, C. 2004. "China's Northeast: From Largest Rust Belt to Fourth Economic Engine?" *China Leadership Monitor* 9: 1–15.

Magaziner, Ira, and Robert Reich. 1983. *Minding America's Business: The Decline and Rise of the American Economy*. New York: Harcourt Brace.

Mallach, Alan, ed. 2012. *Rebuilding Legacy Cities: New Directions for the Industrial Heartland*. New York, NY: The American Assembly.

National Bureau of Economic Research (NBER). 2009. "Business Cycle Expansions and Contractions." Accessed May 14, 2010. http://www.nber.org/cycles.html.

Pallagst, Karina. 2010. "Viewpoint: The Planning Research Agenda: Shrinking Cities – a Challenge for Planning Cultures." *Town Planning Review* 81(5): i–vi.

Pendall, Rolf, Kathryn A. Foster, and Margaret Cowell. 2010. "Resilience and Regions: Building Understanding of the Metaphor." *Cambridge Journal of Regions, Economy and Society* 3(1): 1–14.

Pieper, Ute. 1999. "Deindustrialization and the Social and Economic Sustainability Nexus in Developing Countries: Cross-Country Evidence on Productivity and Employment." Working Paper No. 10, Center for Economic Policy Analysis, New School University.

Power, Anne, Jörg Ploeger, and Astrid Winkler. 2010. *Phoenix Cities: The Fall and Rise of Great Industrial Cities*. Bristol, UK: Policy Press.

Revenga, Ana L. 1992. "Exporting Jobs? The Impact of Import Competition on Employment and Wages in U.S. Manufacturing." *The Quarterly Journal of Economics* 107(1): 255–284.

Ricardo, David. 1821. *On the Principles of Political Economy and Taxation*. London: John Murray.

Rosen, Richard. 1984. "Regional Variations in Employment and Unemployment during 1970–82." *BLS Monthly Labor Review*. Available online: http://bls.gov/opub/mlr/1984/02/art5full.pdf.

Safford, Sean. 2009. *Why the Garden Club Couldn't Save Youngstown: The Transformation of the Rust Belt*. Cambridge, MA: Harvard University Press.

Sassen, Saskia. 1990. "Economic Restructuring and the American City." *Annual Review of Sociology* 16: 465–490.

Savitch, Hank V. 2011. "A Strategy for Neighborhood Decline and Regrowth: Forging the French Connection." *Urban Affairs Review* 47(6): 800–837.

Schilling, Joseph, and Jonathan Logan. 2008. "Greening the Rust Belt: A Green Infrastructure Model for Right Sizing America's Shrinking Cities." *Journal of the American Planning Association* 74(4): 451–466.

Schilling, Joseph, and Alan Mallach. 2012. *Cities in Transition: A Guide for Practicing Planners*. American Planning Association PAS Report. Chicago: APA.

Schoenberger, Erica. 1987. "Technological and Organizational Change in Automobile Production: Spatial Implications." *Regional Studies* 21(3): 199–214.

Singleton, Christopher J. 1992. "Auto Industry Jobs in the 1980s: A Decade of Transition." *Monthly Labor Review* 115(2): 18–27.

Thurow, Lester. 1980. *The Zero-Sum Society*. New York: Basic Books.

Van der Gaag, Nicole, Leo van Wissen, Evert van Imhoff, and Corina Huisman. 1999. *National and Regional Population Trends in the European Union*. Eurostat Working Papers, 3/1999/E/n8.

Varaiya, Pravin, and Michael Wiseman. 1981. "Investment and Employment in Manufacturing in U.S. Metropolitan Areas 1960–1976." *Regional Science and Urban Economics* 11(4): 431–469.

Wilkerson, Isabel. 2010. *The Warmth of Other Suns: The Epic Story of America's Great Migration*. New York: Random House.

Yago, Glenn, Hyman Korman, Sen-Yuan Wu, and Michale Schwartz. 1984. "Investment and Disinvestment in New York, 1960–1980." *Annals of the American Academy of Political and Social Science* 475(1): 28–38.

2 A glimmer of resilience

Though resilience has long been used as a way to describe an individual's response to a specific challenge or traumatic event, its application to places and structures has only lately been explored (Bonanno 2004; Kaplan 1999). Borrowing from ecology, engineering, and psychology, we can see how recent efforts by urban planners and economic developers have brought us nearer to a comprehensive definition of adaptive resilience. To get there, we will explore how resilience has been conceived in other fields and describe how it can be modified for useful application to regions experiencing longer-term challenges like deindustrialization and economic restructuring. The chapter will conclude with a comprehensive definition of adaptive resilience to guide planners, practitioners, policymakers, and other leaders at the local and regional level.

Like the concept of sustainability, the resilience concept has ascended dramatically to its lauded perch in our disciplinary lexicon. In the social sciences, we have already seen the Phoenix rise from the ashes, the poor pulled up by their bootstraps, and the sustainability triangle duplicated *ad infinitum*. In urban studies and urban planning, we have lately become enamored by the concept of resilience and by the idea that both people and places can recover, and sometimes even thrive, in the face of adversity.[1] Recent investigations of urban resilience have found that cities tend to be resilient in the face of natural disasters, meaning that they often revert to their pre-disaster state as measured by tangible indicators like population and jobs, or the slightly more ambiguous concepts of resumed economic activity or regional traffic flow (Vale and Campanella 2005). We have seen plentiful research about resilience in the face of sudden or episodic disruptions but comparatively little about the ability of places to recover in the face of other types of disasters, including the longer-term stress of deindustrialization (Berke and Campanella 2006).[2] Given that resilience remains such an ambiguous, or *fuzzy*, concept, further exploration seems warranted (Markusen 1999; for more on resilience as it relates to fuzziness, see Pendall et al. 2010).

The limitations of ecological and engineering resilience

The concept of resilience has been analyzed and defined differently by scholars across a variety of disciplines, including ecology, psychology, economics, disaster studies, political science, and other fields. We learn from ecologists and engineers that there are two main types of resilience: *ecological resilience*, which describes instances in which some sort of disruption pushes a system from one equilibrium to another; and *engineering resilience*, which pertains to instances in which a system returns to its presumed steady state after a disruption (Berkes and Folke 1998, 12). It is this second definition that has been utilized most often by fields that are associated with urban planning because it emphasizes the recovery of people and places in the wake of some specific shock or prolonged stress (Pickett et al. 2004; Vale and Campanella 2005).

In order to understand these main approaches to resilience, it is useful to think about the two main types of challenges that regions face: disasters, which generally happen once and often rather quickly; and slow burns or slow-moving crises, which unfold gradually over time. Studies of responses to disasters (e.g., hurricane, flood, tornado, tsunami), which often use the engineering version of resilience, tend to focus on the ability of a city or region to recover its population, economy, or built form (Vale and Campanella 2005). A city or region that is resilient in the face of a disaster would therefore be one that resumed its growth trajectory or previous functions after a brief disruption (Pendall et al. 2010).

Researchers studying a city or region's response to a slow burn or slow-moving crisis (e.g., economic restructuring, influx of immigrants) might also utilize the ecological resilience framework to better understand the transformation of systems as they adapt over longer periods of time. Instead of looking for a quick 'return to normalcy,' researchers of slow-moving crises might look for a region that, in the face of a slow burn, has either improved on the outcome being measured, or at least not worsened, since the previous time period (Pendall et al. 2010). Depending on the variable being considered, we might benchmark a region's resilience by the length of time needed to resume a gradual decrease in unemployment or poverty.

Slow-burn challenges tend to naturally correspond to ideas about path dependence and lock-in, two concepts that are often mentioned in the economics literature. Research in institutional economics, macroeconomics, and political science has focused on systems that are ostensibly stuck at a sub-optimal level, a phenomenon sometimes called 'lock-in.' Also called path dependence, this phenomenon is thought to be the result of "institutional tissues"; which include both organizations or other formal structures and ideas that pattern behavior and establish norms, rules and laws (Hassink 2005). Over time, these institutional tissues are thought to discourage restructuring or reorganization by obstructing entrepreneurs in a multitude of arenas. The lock-in that often results is a consequence or manifestation of path dependence and has strong implications for a region's (or person's or company's) resilience (Redding, 2002).

In many cases we can look back and see that a system, at any given point in time, had numerous paths to choose from and little knowledge about the implications of choosing any one of the available paths. At that same point in time a series of decisions are made that allow one technological or political regime to come to the fore. Human systems begin to fall into place, reflecting and responding to that technological or political regime. Social, physical, economic, and cultural infrastructure follows suit, making a continuation of that development path seem all but inevitable. As the system becomes locked into this pathway, human systems increasingly believe "that only a massive or radical shock or stress is enough to motivate pathbreaking behaviors and changes" (Pendall et al. 2010, 76).

Numerous examples have been used in the economics literature to illustrate path dependence. A commonly cited case is the continued use of the QWERTY keyboard despite known inefficiencies. The QWERTY keyboard was developed first but was quickly challenged by August Dvorak's more efficient keyboard system. Despite widely documented improvements in efficiency, Dvorak's keyboard was never adopted. Paul David (1985) has argued "competition in the absence of perfect futures markets drove the industry prematurely into standardization *on the wrong system* – where decentralized decision making subsequently has sufficed to hold it" (David 1985, 336). A decentralized decision-making process, as well as strong technical connectedness scale economies, and irreversibility due to learning and habituation are the main reasons why Dvorak's more efficient keyboard arrangement was never adopted and the QWERTY keyboard remains.

Institutional economists and macroeconomists have found that if a product, company, or process is initially successful, then increasing returns may reinforce that initial advantage and the product, company or process may then proceed towards complete domination or 'lock-in' of the industry. Related to 'lock-in' is the theory of cumulative advantage and disadvantage, which social scientists use to describe how an initial comparative advantage or disadvantage of resources can lead to successive incremental gains or losses that are often without merit (see David 1985; Puffert 2002; and Cusumano et al. 1992). Such a definition is important in the study of regions, where initial gains or losses can exacerbate the original comparative condition, thereby causing a snowball effect that may increase the gap between the haves and the have-nots.

Political scientists have also researched the persistence of sub-optimal institutional arrangements. Although they call this phenomenon 'lock-in,' they differ from the economists in that they associate it with both positive and negative connotations. Hassink (2005) suggests that lock-in results from "institutional tissues," which "consist both of organizations ('formal structures with an explicit purpose'), such as political administrations at all spatial levels, trade unions, large enterprises and business support agencies, and 'things that pattern behavior' such as norms, rules and laws" (Hassink 2005, 523, referring to Edquist 1997, 27). Woodlief (1998) has found that at the city level governments can often get locked into sub-optimal policies that are made during times of great uncertainty. He argues that such lock-in happens because the institutional stickiness of a city's policy-making environment generally renders policies resistant to change and because most of the people involved have reason to resist change in the status quo. Such institutional tissues are especially important at the regional scale, where they are, in the absence of more formalized arrangements, sometimes the only source of supra-local cohesiveness in existence.

In the end, none of these traditional conceptualizations of resilience or path dependence is appropriate for the type of research being conducted here. When regional actors develop a response to deindustrialization, they aren't looking to achieve (or maintain) a new equilibrium, nor are they looking to simply 'bounce back' to their pre-challenge state. Regional resilience is not synonymous with accepting or embracing a new equilibrium, especially if that new equilibrium just means the sub-par status quo of the post-challenge period. Regional actors ought not to be satisfied with a new equilibrium that includes a higher unemployment rate or greater inequity amongst residents, both of which are common features of a post-disaster state (Kumar 2011; Liu and Plyer 2010). Simply stated, urban planners and policymakers are not likely pleased when a disruption or challenge sends a region into a new, less desirable equilibrium. Similarly, they are also not likely supportive when their regions lock into inefficient paths.

At the same time, regional resilience is also not just 'bouncing back' to a region's pre-challenge state, especially if that state was less than desirable to begin with. More importantly, a 'return to normal' in the face of global restructuring would not be possible in most cases anyway. The engineering view of resilience is therefore imperfect in that it is concerned only with how fast or how easily a region 'bounces back' or recovers from a particular challenge. Such a framework says nothing about the trade-offs associated with 'bouncing back' and nothing about how regional actors might prepare themselves to deal with future problems or might learn from the mistakes they have made in response to a given challenge. Instead, engineering resilience corresponds to the speed with which a region returns to its 'normal' or pre-challenge state, veritably ignoring the concepts of adaptation, preparation, or experiential learning.

Similar problems have also been identified in the path dependence literature. Just as regional leaders are not likely comfortable with an engineering or ecological resilience view, most would probably cringe at the idea of their region being locked into an inefficient path, and especially at the idea that 'institutional stickiness' would be used as an excuse for why they should resist change.

Towards adaptive resilience

A review of recent research confirms that there clearly are tensions among and between different conceptualizations and measures of resilience. It would be imprudent to suggest then that there is any one real measure of regional resilience or any one optimal regional state, as both the measure and the state will depend on the problem at hand and the type of region being considered (Christopherson 2010).

One way to help clarify our discussion of resilience is to think about regions as complex adaptive systems. Rather than merely striving for a return to normalcy or a resumption of pre-challenge behaviors or outcomes, an adaptive system refers to an entity, like a metropolitan region, that has the ability to change or adapt in response to stresses and strains (Carpenter et al. 2005). In such systems, resilience is not related to equilibrium, a return to 'normal,' or even to resilient outcomes; it is instead a "*dynamic attribute associated with a process of continual development*" (Pendall et al. 2010). Across Rust Belt regions, where decades of restructuring have eroded any sense of 'normalcy,' it is this adaptive systems perspective of resilience that seems most applicable. As large users of resources outside their formal boundaries, regions are also inherently open systems, interacting and adapting to systems geographically outside of them (Martin-Breen and Anderies 2011).

In order to capture this sense of interactive process and continual development, adaptive resilience is most often explained through the use of a 'figure-8' diagram, which depicts the four phases of a region's adaptive cycle as it adjusts to internal and external challenges (for more on the adaptive cycle, see Holling et al. 2002). Each of the four phases – conservation, release, reorganization, and exploitation – relates to the process of adaptive resilience exhibited by the system's susceptibility to stresses or shocks (Figure 2.1). Rather than saying that a region is or is not resilient, the adaptive system model tells us that *resilience levels vary depending on how the region adapts to changes and how it cycles through these four phases*. The adaptive cycle also accounts for two additional aspects of change: a system's potential, meaning the accumulated resources available to a system, and a system's connectedness, which refers to the extent and strength of internal links between a system's actors (Pendall et al. 2010).

Any given region or system will experience varying levels of resilience, depending on where it is within the four-phase cycle. Each quadrant denotes a unique phase and each phase reflects the characteristics of a system or a region and describes the level and direction of resilience at a given moment in time. Thus, a system's resilience levels differ in each phase, as do its stability and certainty. If we think about a hypothetical Midwestern region at the beginning of the 1970s and before deindustrialization unfolds, we would likely begin by discussing the regional system's 'conservation' phase. At this stage, we could imagine that the regional system is accumulating resources and exhibits a fair amount of confidence and an increasingly rigid set of economic structures as many of its older industries are on the cusp of maturity. A few years later, as deindustrialization begins to unfold and flexibility decreases, we might expect to see a corresponding decrease in resilience and increase in vulnerability of the system to an external shock or stress. In some cases, the stress or strain of deindustrialization may be enough to push a regional system from 'conservation' to 'release.' The release stage, much like Schumpeter's

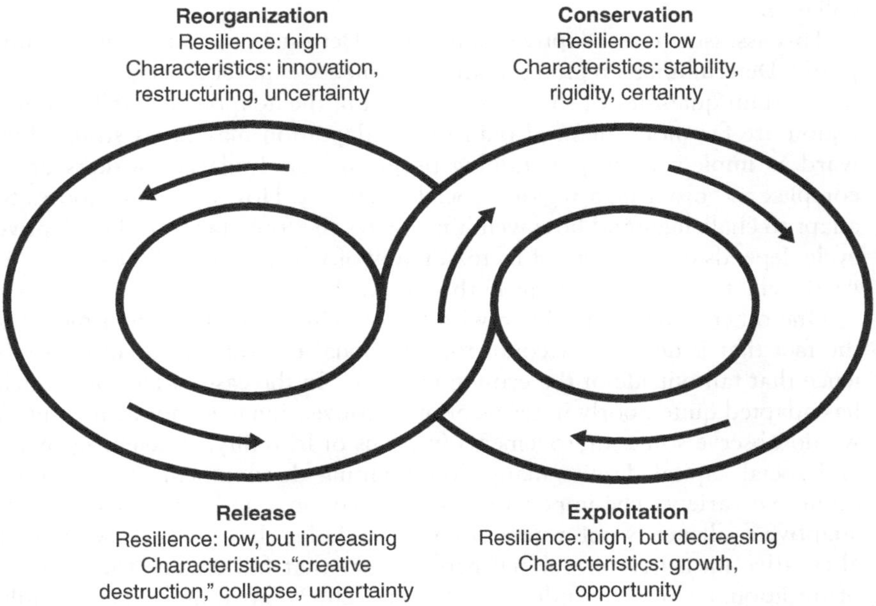

Figure 2.1 Four-phase cycle of system adaptation and change

Source: Pendall et al. (2010), adapted from Holling et al. (2002).

(1975) depiction of creative destruction, would likely include collapse and uncertainty as the region deals with widespread unemployment due to the closure of firms and the increasing obsolescence of mature technologies. During the 'release' phase resilience is low but increases gradually as regional leaders start to assess the problem and begin weighing their options. 'Reorganization' then becomes possible if the regional system begins experimenting and starts to reorganize in response to the stresses of deindustrialization. During 'reorganization,' when creativity and innovation peak and preliminary adaptations begin to take shape, we can expect to see resilience and uncertainty peak as well. Although resilience remains high during the 'exploitation' phase, it begins to decrease as the creative ideas become opportunities and new firms start to solidify. Later on, as these new industries and firms mature and rigidity increases, we see the cycle begin again (Cowell 2013).

If we think of Detroit as an example of a regional system, it seems appropriate to say that the Detroit region has long hovered between the lower-level resilience phases of conservation and release. As we will see in Chapter 5, the region experienced a relatively long period of conservation as automobile production soared in the early part of the twentieth century. Later on, as domestic automobile producers faced greater challenges, the region experienced release, resulting in a protracted period of uncertainty and collapse.

This assessment of adaptive resilience in Detroit is, of course, overly simplistic. Determining a region's adaptive resilience is never as easy as pointing to a certain quadrant of the figure-8 diagram; the adaptive capabilities of a region are far more nuanced than that. Adaptation may be as straightforward as implementing job training programs for displaced workers or as complex as bolstering a region's social safety net. How a region chooses to adapt to challenges and how well it navigates the four stages of the adaptive cycle depends on a variety of factors, many of which will be discussed vis-à-vis the eight case study regions in this book.

One other potential problem with the one-dimensional figure-8 model is the fact that it does not account for additional measures of adaptive resilience that fall outside of the economic sphere. In the case of Detroit, which has adapted quite poorly in terms of most conventional economic measures, we do observe some improvements in terms of livability, civic engagement, and social capital despite many disappointing developments of the more economic variety. The importance of non-economic measures in studies of adaptive resilience is not a new discovery. Scholars have found a variety of alternative measures of regional performance that fall outside the purview of traditional economic indicators. Stiglitz (2002) has found that "broadly participatory processes (such as 'voice,' openness, and transparency)" contribute to sustained regional health (163). Similarly, Pastor et al. (2009) have argued that regional resilience is increasingly determined by business and community-group efforts coalescing around issues of regional equity, including infrastructure, housing, and workforce development. Others have found that these traditional locational factors are necessary pre-conditions, and softer quality-of-life factors like community image and identity may provide supplementary, optimal conditions for regional performance (Wong 2001). As qualitative data suggest below, these non-economic measures tell a very important part of the region's story and indicate that adaptive resilience may in fact reveal itself beyond the facade of traditional economic indicators and a simple, one-dimensional figure-8 diagram.

Another potential shortcoming is that the perceived adaptive resilience of a given region will likely differ based upon who is measuring it and what they are measuring it with. For instance, a corporate executive might see increased productivity or greater market share in the face of international competition as adaptive resilience. Whereas a union official might disagree, seeing the preservation of jobs as more important. A local politician, who is duly concerned with preserving jobs in her or his constituency, will probably also care about city revenues. Thus, each of these actors may assess a region's adaptive resilience by his or her own set of indicators, including: job growth; productivity growth in terms of value added per job; increased market share; preservation of union jobs; and others. Sometimes these types of outcomes may in fact be at odds with one another. For instance, in the case of Detroit, a General Motors (GM) official, who is really only concerned with increasing market share, does not necessarily care whether production jobs remain in metropolitan Detroit or even whether the region as a whole will prosper in the long run; he or she probably only cares that quality GM automobiles are being produced as quickly and efficiently as possible. On the other hand, a local public official – who once may have cared about market share because of the historical correlation between GM's success and metropolitan Detroit's prosperity – is probably now more concerned with keeping GM and other high-paying jobs in his or her jurisdiction than with whether or not GM's market share is increasing. Hence, in a one-dimensional depiction of adaptive resilience, we can see how there might be divergence in terms of what each actor sees as adaptive resilience.

Because of these shortcomings and because of its imprecise nature, the figure-8 diagram has sometimes been replaced by a depiction of adaptive resilience as a series of nested figure-8s (Figure 2.2). The nested figure-8 depiction stems from the idea that regions are complex systems that function not just

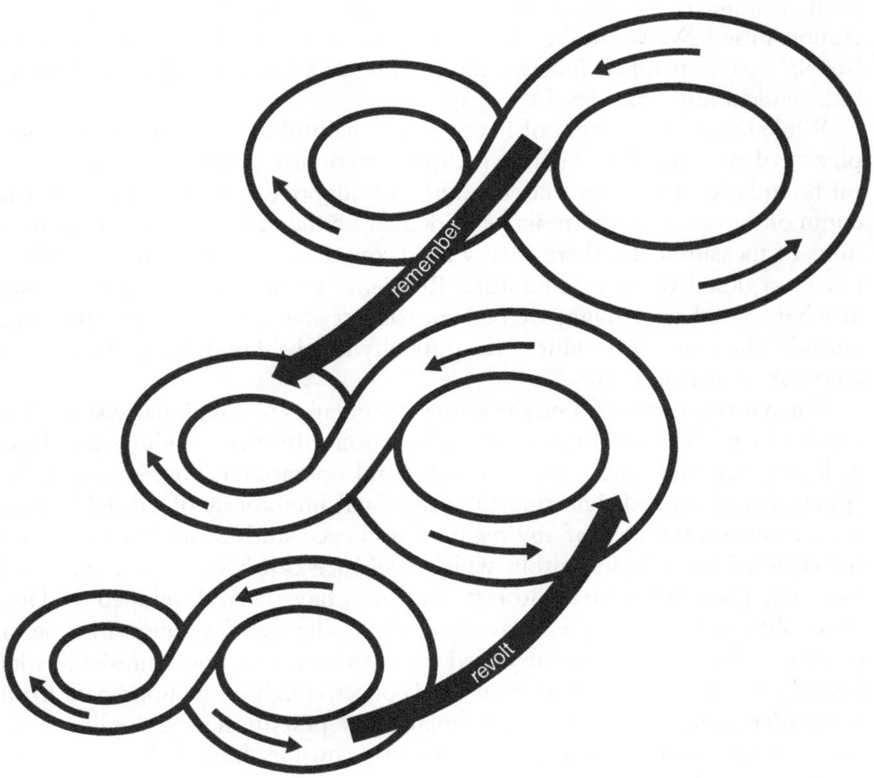

Figure 2.2 Four-phase nested cycle of system adaptation and change
Source: Pendall et al. (2010), adapted from Holling et al. (2002)

in one predictable cycle but rather as a series of interconnected cycles that interact with each other to create a more nuanced series of outcomes and processes. These processes are multiscalar and multidimensional, can proceed at different speeds, and can occur over vastly different timeframes.

As Pendall et al. (2010) describe, the nested system is inherently applicable to regions in that it incorporates both a 'revolt' function for smaller subsystems and a 'remember' function for larger subsystems. Smaller systems may influence or react to disruptions by 'revolting' against larger systems. For example, if the regional system does not exhibit adaptive resilience, vacancy and abandonment in one block may cause a smaller-scale 'revolt' to spread to larger neighborhood areas or even to citywide swaths. On the other hand, the 'remember' function may allow larger systems to stabilize the smaller, 'revolting' subsystems within a region. As Swanstrom et al. (2009) note, a stable and diverse economy could help a system 'remember' or mitigate the cascading effects of vacancy and abandonment within smaller systems. However, too much of the 'remember' function could also present a problem for a regional system. Responses may become routinized and increasingly rigid, meaning that the flexibility of the system and its ability to adapt may be compromised. We would be wise then to encourage the development of both 'revolt' and 'remember' functionality, but to do so in a way that is relatively independent and multi-level by design.

While the nested system of figure-8s is a helpful way to convey the complexity of systems, it does ignore the question of how geographic and temporal boundaries affect our understanding of adaptive resilience. Though it is common in research and practice to deliberate the most appropriate unit or units of measurement, there is very little consensus on this within the adaptive or regional resilience literature. Resilience scholars will commonly ask: at what spatial scale might we best measure resilience? And over what time period? These questions hint at the difficulty involved in defining the parameters for resilience studies.

When it comes to defining the spatial boundaries of a regional system, it is important to think about how our delineations affect our findings and how well they actually reflect the functional and operational boundaries of the system being studied. Ignoring the functional limitations of available data for a moment, the goal of any regional resilience study would be to specify the regional boundaries within which resilience can best be perceived and assessed. Though no hard and fast guidelines have been developed to date, we could imagine that questions about the resilience of a region in time of economic duress might be answered using the regional commuteshed as its boundary. An environmental or cultural concern might draw upon data from a broader ecological footprint. Scholars and practitioners grappling with these questions would be wise to judiciously consider how their spatial definitions affect the observation and measurement of resilience.

And when it comes to temporal boundaries, we must consider how starting and ending points also affect observations and assessments of regional resilience. How much time should we allot for a region to engage in recovery before we assess its resilience? How long before and after an event should we look for the identification of trends or patterns? How do we account for different temporal norms, both in terms of differences across regions and in terms of different types of challenges? Much like the geographic boundary questions above, questions of time will also depend on the nature of the challenge. While an abrupt shock like a hurricane or blizzard might require only a few months or years of data, a chronic or longer-term challenge like deindustrialization may require decades and maybe even a whole century's worth of data in order for us to observe and assess adaptive resilience. Still, some others may require projection data of future scenarios in order to assess how well a region has adapted to a particular longer-term challenge. As with any study, the choices we make about boundaries and unit of analysis in resilience analyses must be deliberated in a thoughtful and constructive manner.

It is in the context of this warning that Davoudi (2012) urges us to conceive of adaptive resilience as a continually changing process that should be considered "not as a being, but as a becoming" (304). Resilience in this interpretation is therefore not a fixed asset so much as it is *performed* when complex systems confront a significant challenge. Performance seems fitting as a way to frame this particular analysis of economic development responses to deindustrialization. Much like a performance, each region's individual economic development responses were brainstormed, written, and executed by a diverse group of actors, all of whom were influenced by their own training, experiences, and personal characteristics and beliefs. It is therefore important that we consider how the cast in these performances affects the process and outcomes in these regions.

Related to resilience as performance is the idea that systems may also have the capability to self-organize and exhibit *novelty* in the face of a challenge. In light of a severe challenge, most communities or regions have some ability to organize themselves to craft a response. Some scholars have argued that this response is *novel*, meaning that it cannot be predicted or pre-designed (Martin-Breen and Anderies 2011). To be sure, some degree of self-organization is latent or ongoing. Thus, the truly novel response involves experimentation and innovation in real-time but relies on assets and infrastructure already in place. If novelty is indeed an important characteristic of a system's adaptive resilience, leaders would be wise to foster novel behavior, people, and institutions within their region. Together, their collective novelty may offer a more effective way to self-organize when normal mechanisms of response are disrupted during crisis (Gunderson and Holling 2002). However, recent work on this subject has warned that the capacity to self-organize – to sense, interdict, and intervene in times of challenge – cannot be simply imposed from above, but instead "must be nurtured in the social structures and relationships that govern people's everyday lives" (Zolli and Healy 2012).

To conceive of a region's response as a performance or novelty that derives from nurturing and support moves us much closer to a more useful understanding of adaptive resilience, which inherently builds upon the regional resilience literature as well as ecological and engineering resilience principles. To incorporate the performance and novelty elements as well as the complexity of an adaptive system, we must forge a new definition for regions experiencing a prolonged challenge. To that end, it makes sense to say that *adaptive resilience is observed in regions when they conscientiously, proactively, and continually respond to a challenge, and do so in a way that improves the chances for a healthy region in the longer term.* If we consider adaptation and transformation as regional capabilities, it then becomes possible for researchers, policymakers, and practitioners to identify the circumstances and mediations that allow a region to exhibit adaptive resilience.

Adaptive resilience and 'good outcomes'

Assessing the performance of a regional system broadly, including the innovative ways in which it responds to challenge, moves us toward a more robust, albeit complex, understanding of adaptive resilience. One way to refine our understanding is to envision a set of hypothetical 'good outcomes' that would act as barometers of a region's adaptive response to a given challenge. Though there are no hard and fast rules about how a region *should* recover from a challenge, the presence of good outcomes would suggest that a region has navigated the challenge well, and the absence of good outcomes would suggest that it has not been as successful in its navigation of the challenge. Depending on the subject matter of interest, these good outcomes might focus on the environment, society as a whole or individual persons, infrastructural systems, among others.

For the purposes of this study, the relatively narrow focus will be on regional demographic, economy, and equity outcomes, as they are most closely related to the goals of economic and community development plans and policies. Borrowing from Foster (2006), who examined the resilience of Buffalo, we find a number of ways in which 'good outcomes' relate to adaptive resilience. In terms of demographics, our quest to uncover 'good outcomes' urges us to ask whether the population for the region as a whole stabilized or increased as the region adapted to the challenge at hand. At a more micro level, we also want to know whether there is an equitable distribution of people between city and suburbs and whether or not the region is racially integrated. In terms of the economy, we would want to know whether employment levels and rates have stabilized or improved over time and whether per capita income has improved for people in the region. And finally, in terms of equity, we would want to know whether the poverty rate has improved over time. Through a combination of quantitative data in Chapter 4 and qualitative data in Chapters 5 and 6, answers to these questions for each region are discussed below. In the meantime, we can say that there is evidence of adaptive resilience and 'good outcomes' in the face of deindustrialization if: a region has a stable, equitably distributed, and racially integrated population base; a stable or improving unemployment rate; improving per capita income; and declining but equitably distributed poverty.

If we think about adaptation and response as a means to achieving these 'good outcomes' throughout the adaptive cycle, we must also ask another set of questions about the actors and the decisions that they make. To gauge a given region's movement through the adaptive cycle, it is essential to ask whether regional leaders have responded in a way that improves the chances for a healthy region in the long run. Have regional leaders incorporated broad community input when crafting their response? Have they drawn upon the strength of the region or have they increased divisiveness? Do they continue to learn from their past mistakes and from their successes? Have they used this information to increase employment opportunities for residents, improve the educational system, invest in sustainable transit, and/or increase regional equity? How have they adjusted to the realities of changing population and employment levels? Knowing how each region fares in light of these questions assists us in locating each region's position within the four stages of the figure-8 diagram.

Being able to identify the quadrant or phase that best describes each case study region in the wake of deindustrialization goes a long way in telling how and how well each region adapted to the trials of deindustrialization. The challenge then becomes figuring out why regions experience the adaptive cycle in different ways. How do some regions 'turn the corner' between conservation and release or between reorganization and exploitation? Does 'turning the corner' necessarily result in 'good outcomes'? Why do some regions remain in the conservation quadrant longer than others?

Answering all of these questions is outside of the scope of this study, but they remain important because they remind us of the importance of spending time to identify actors and their underlying motivations and assumptions. Furthermore, these questions also lend weight to the idea that there are many ways to understand adaptive regional resilience in the wake of a long-term challenge, including conventional economic measures and indicators of a less economic variety. In subsequent chapters, both types of measures will be examined vis-à-vis each case study region's economic development response to deindustrialization. Conclusions based upon these measures will help us to identify how each region used economic development planning to adapt over time and how its actions relate to the four phases of the figure-8 diagram. We begin that process in the next chapter with a discussion about the range of economic development responses available to these regions.

Notes

1 The Building Resilient Regions (BRR) network, a MacArthur Foundation-sponsored research effort of which I am a member, examines the role of governance and other factors in shaping regional resilience outcomes in the face of long-term region-scale economic and social challenges (http://brr.berkeley.edu).

2 Other BRR network participants have engaged in economic analyses related to regional economic capacity, economic shocks, and economic resilience. Their efforts have focused primarily on shorter-term and more recent economic shocks. For more on this work, see Blumenthal et al. (2009).

References

Berke, Philip R., and Thomas J. Campanella. 2006. "Planning for Postdisaster Resiliency." *The Annals of the American Academy of Political and Social Science* 604(1): 192–207.

Berkes, Fikret, and Carl Folke. 1998. *Linking Social and Ecological Systems: Management Practices and Social Mechanisms for Building Resilience*. New York: Cambridge University Press.

Blumenthal, Pamela, Harold Wolman, and Edward Hill. 2009. "Understanding the Economic Performance of Metropolitan Areas in the United States." *Urban Studies* 46(3): 605–627.

Bonanno, George A. 2004. "Loss, Trauma, and Human Resilience: Have We Underestimated the Human Capacity to Thrive After Extremely Aversive Events?" *American Psychologist* 59(1): 20–28.

Carpenter, Stephen R., Frances Westley, and Monica Turner. 2005. "Surrogates for Resilience of Social-ecological Systems." *Ecosystems* 8(8): 941–944.

Christopherson, Susan. 2010. "Never Let a Good Crisis Go to Waste: Re-Imagining Resilience in the Light of the Great Recession." *Critical Planning Theory* 17(Summer): 108–123.

Cowell, Margaret. 2013. "Bounce Back of Move On: Regional Resilience and Economic Development Planning." *Cities* 30: 212–222.

Cusumano, Michael A., Yiorgos Mylonadis, and Richard S. Rosenbloom. 1992. "Strategic Maneuvering and Mass-Market Dynamics: The Triumph of VHS over Beta." *The Business History Review* 66 (1): 51–94.

David, Paul A. 1985. "CLIO and the Economics of QWERTY" *The American Economic Review* 75(2): 332–327.

Davoudi, Simin. 2012. '"Resilience: A Bridging Concept or a Dead End?" Planning Theory & Practice' 13(2): 228–333.

Edquist, Charles. 1997. "Systems of Innovation Approaches – Their Emergence and Characteristics." In *Systems of Innovation: Technologies, Institutions and Organizations*, edited by Charles Edquist, 1–35. London/Washington, DC: Pinter.

Foster, Kathryn. 2006. "A Case Study Approach to Understanding Regional Resilience." Working Paper 2007–08. University of California (November).

Gunderson, Lance, and C.S. Holling, eds. 2002. *Panarchy: Understanding Transformations in Human and Natural Systems*. Washington, DC: Island Press.

Hassink, Robert. 2005. "How to Unlock Regional Economies from Path Dependency? From Learning Region to Learning Cluster." *European Planning Studies* 13(4): 521–535.

Holling, C.S., Lance H. Gunderson, and Garry D. Peterson. 2002. "Sustainability and Panarchies," In *Panarchy: Understanding Transformations in Human and Natural Systems*, edited by L. H. Gunderson and C.S. Holling, 63–102. Washington, DC: Island Press.

Kaplan, Howard B. 1999. "Toward an Understanding of Resilience: A Critical Review of Definitions and Models." In *Resilience and Development: Positive Life*

Adaptations, edited by Meyer D. Glantz and Jeannette L. Johnson, 17–83. New York: Kluwer Academic/Plenum.

Kumar, Mukesh. 2011. "A Tale of Uneven Comebacks: Community Planning and Neighborhood Design on the Mississippi Gulf Coast." In *Resilience and Opportunity:* Lessons from the U.S. Gulf Coast after Katrina and Rita, edited by Amy Liu, Roland V. Anglin, Richard M. Mizzelle Jr., and Allison Plyer, 148–160. Washington, DC: Brookings Institution.

Liu, Amy, and Allison Plyer. 2010. "An Overview of Greater New Orleans: From Recovery to Transformation" In The New Orleans Index at Five. Washington, DC: Brookings Institution and Greater New Orleans Community Data Center.

Markusen, Ann. 1999. "Fuzzy Concepts, Scanty Evidence, Policy Distance: The Case for Rigour and Policy Relevance in Critical Regional Studies." *Regional Studies* 33(9): 701–717.

Martin-Breen, Patrick, and J. Marty Anderies. 2011. *Resilience: A Literature Review.* Rockefeller Foundation Working Paper.

Pastor, Manuel, Chris Brenner, and Martha Matsuoka. 2009. *This Could be the Start of Something Big: How Social Movements for Regional Equity are Reshaping Metropolitan America.* Ithaca, NY: Cornell University Press.

Pendall, Rolf, Kathryn Foster, and Margaret Cowell. 2010. "Resilience and Regions: Building Understanding of the Metaphor." *Cambridge Journal of Regions, Economy and Society* 3(1): 71–84.

Pickett, Steward T.A., Mary Cadenasso, and Morgan Grove. 2004. "Resilient Cities: Meaning, Models, and Metaphor for Integrating the Ecological, Socio-economic, and Planning Realms." *Landscape and Urban Planning* 69: 369–384.

Puffert, Douglas J. 2002. "Path Dependence in Spatial Networks: The Standardization of Railway Track Gauge." *Explorations in Economic History* 39: 282–314.

Redding, Stephen. 2002. "Path Dependence, Endogenous Innovation, and Growth." *International Economic Review* 43(4): 1215–1248.

Schumpeter, Joseph. 1975. *Capitalism, Socialism and Democracy.* New York: Harper.

Stiglitz, Joseph E. 2002. "Participation and Development: Perspectives from the Comprehensive Development Paradigm." *Review of Development Economics* 6(2): 163–182.

Swanstrom, Todd, Karen Chapple, and Dan Immergluck. 2009. "Regional Resilience in the Face of Foreclosures: Evidence from Six Metropolitan Areas." Working Paper 2009–05. University of California (May).

Vale, Lawrence J., and Thomas H. Campanella, eds. 2005. *The Resilient City: How Modern Cities Recover from Disaster.* New York: Oxford University Press.

Wong, Cecelia. 2001. "The Relationship between Quality of Life and Local Economic Development: An Empirical Study of Local Authority Areas in England." *Cities* 18(1): 25–32.

Woodlief, Anthony. 1998. "The Path-Dependent City." *Urban Affairs Review* 33(3): 405–437.

Zolli, Andrew and Ann Marie Healy. 2012. *Resilience: Why Things Bounce Back.* New York: Free Press.

3 Enter the economic developers

While Rust Belt regions grappled with deindustrialization during the 1970s and 1980s, economic development during that period also became increasingly difficult for another reason: a simultaneous shift in the way that economic development was conceived, funded, and executed. At the national scale, the late 1970s and early 1980s brought a change in focus from federal initiatives to more local- and state-based practices as well as increased public-private partnerships. The impetus for this shift came largely from the Republicans in power at the time, many of whom called for widespread deregulation and decentralization of numerous government services, including most economic development initiatives. New public-private partnerships generally placed greater emphasis on creating a good and attractive business climate and moved away from previous concerns with inner-city poverty alleviation and equitable development. Accordingly, the tools used for economic development began to shift from federal and state entitlement programs to local and regional incentives, subsidies, business assistance, as well as the banking and development of land.

As these changes took shape, Midwestern regions began responding in various ways. In some regions, economic development remained largely within the policy realm, involving policy-driven agendas focused on annexation and increasingly popular relocation incentives. In other regions, economic development emphasized planning or visioning processes in order to set the agenda and tone for future regional development. Below I consider how the evolution of economic development policy and practice informed the regional responses to restructuring during this period but first I begin with a more general discussion of urban political economy and how it relates to economic development.

Urban political economy

Much can be gleaned from the urban political economy literature of the 1970s and 1980s. In a series of overlapping debates, political scientists worked through numerous ideas about the relationship between community, politics, and social theory. Most accounts of these debates begin with Ira

Katznelson's 1981 book, *City Trenches*. In his study of the overlap between community politics and social theory, Katznelson describes the effect that mass urban movements of the mid-twentieth century had on urban areas and in particular New York City's Washington Heights neighborhood. In studying the politics of community participation in this neighborhood, Katznelson argues that studies of class formation, which typically focus only on the workplace, are much stronger if they consider also the community at large and the relationship between it and the workplace.

The concern for local urban politics is also manifest in Mollenkopf's *The Contested City* (1983). Mollenkopf's work on growth coalitions begins by disavowing the two main arguments used to describe the structure of political power: neo-Marxism and pluralism (9). Instead, Mollenkopf argues that political entrepreneurs built pro-growth coalitions out of conflicting interests, using politics and government as driving forces to override diverse economic and social interests. Though the author's use of Boston and San Francisco as case studies is extremely useful in furthering his ideas about the political entrepreneur's role in the growth coalition, Mollenkopf's most relevant contribution to the deindustrialization literature is the typology that he develops. Mollenkopf attempts to sort America's largest cities into three main categories:

1 distressed cities, like Newark or Gary, which are often in the Northeast and tend to be old, declining industrial cities that have few administrative and service activities but rich legacies of labor, racial, and neighborhood conflict;
2 mixed cities, like Boston and San Francisco, that have rising administrative and service activities which have been promoted by pro-growth politics and have experienced some conflict over urban development; and
3 newer cities, like those in the Southwest, which have stronger service centers and branch plants but little traditional industry and experience little conflict or political debate over growth issues (217).

Such a typology, one of the first of its kind, is useful in thinking about the ways in which certain policies have shaped outcomes in cities with common characteristics. This typology, and the comparative framework exemplified by the Boston and San Francisco cases Mollenkopf conducted, set the stage for many of the mixed method analyses of urban growth coalitions that would follow.

A slight contrast to the ideas proposed in Mollenkopf's *The Contested City* is provided in Fainstein and Fainstein's edited book, *Restructuring the City: The Political Economy of Urban Development* (1983). Focusing specifically on urban regime theory, much of their book focuses on the comparison of five main case studies: Denver, Detroit, New Haven, New Orleans, and San Francisco. Each case is presented by a different author, but redevelopment seen through the lens of urban political economy is the focus throughout. The message overall is that redevelopment is pivotal in the relationship between local and national forces (vii). The chapters written by the Fainsteins are perhaps the most useful contribution to the discourse on redevelopment because they simultaneously stress the ability of non-elite groups to infiltrate state development processes and make known the effects that federal policy has on the urban and local political economy.

Stemming from the expansive urban-focused work of Katznelson, Mollenkopf, Fainstein and Fainstein, and others, there emerged a series of powerful movements within the political economy literature that would indelibly shape the way that we think and learn about cities, and also regions. One of the most powerful trajectories resulting from their work is a group of scholars concerned with the definition of and careful consideration of the 'growth machine,' which is generally thought to be a coalition of business elites and local public officials in the pursuit of economic development (Molotch 1976). In thinking about how economic development decisions were being made at the local level, many researchers began to grapple with the intersection between the growth machine or coalition and the local growth ideology (see Swanstrom 1985; DiGaetano and Klemanski 1993; Feagin 1988; Gottdeiner 1985). The application of the growth coalition hypothesis to deindustrializing urban areas was particularly useful in thinking about the relationship between increasingly mobile world capital and local economic development efforts (Bluestone and Harrison 1982; Horan and Jonas 1998).

Most accounts about growth coalitions begin with John Logan and Harvey Molotch's (1987) tome, *Urban Fortunes: The Political Economy of Place*. Their argument builds on Peterson's (1981) work, which found that urban politicians are primarily concerned with increasing economic growth and are therefore often complicit with outside investors. Logan and Molotch describe the growth machine as a coalition of elites with common interests in real estate development who use local institutions, politics, and culture to intensify land use and reap financial gain. Others describe these elite actors as the *rentiers*, an exclusive group of people who seek to increase the exchange value of land, as opposed to the rest of the population who value property as a living or work space (Judge, Stoker, and Wolman 1995). It stands that the *rentiers* typically enjoy(ed) close relationships with the political elite, which led to a synergetic relationship that would drive most policy outcomes. Logan and Molotch optimistically add community residents to this mix of urban politicians and outside investors as part of the decision-making process. They are, however, quick to note that members of the growth coalition generally exclude community residents from the urban development process. Such exclusion can result in long-term detrimental impacts on community members and small business owners, in stark contrast to the 'value-free development' growth coalition ideology that says all growth is good.

Pushing back against the notion of value-free economic development in the 1980s, Cox and Mair (1988) highlighted the ill-effects associated with the growing competition seen among localities in the wake of economic restructuring. Their main assertion is that local business coalitions coalesce around the idea of warding off opposition to local economic development plans by co-opting their potential rivals and building a "consensus in which the politics of restructuring local economies is conceived of as a competition among 'localities' rather than as a struggle within them" (307–308). A similar argument, which is also accompanied by empirical evidence, is made by Moore and Squires (1991), who argue that the conservative ideology of privatism emphasizes the necessity of local capital accumulation. In their examination of Kenosha, Wisconsin, the authors describe the uneven development that arose in the aftermath of a Chrysler plant closing in that city. Such uneven development, seen as resulting from growth coalition initiatives, caused selected sectors, neighborhoods, and population subgroups to unfairly bear the costs of the economic restructuring and subsequent (re) development. In the end, the authors find that "The organization of a political coalition that can effectively challenge the ideology of privatism depends upon more than the recognition of common interests. It also depends upon local and national developments that give legitimacy to innovative public policies" (172).

In their analysis of deindustrialization and restructuring in Flint, Michigan, Lord and Price (1992) found that local leaders took a dual approach to redevelopment in the aftermath of restructuring: they utilized tax abatements to induce GM and other manufacturing firms to stay, and focused on tourism development to diversify their tax base. Through interviews and document analysis, the authors concluded that both liberal and conservative adherents to the growth ideology were happy with such an approach because it satisfied, at least in part, their respective broader goals of projected job growth for the urban underclass and capital accumulation through tourism-based construction contracts and related small business spin-offs (166). The authors, however, advocate a more progressive alternative to the growth ideology, arguing instead that a national policy to address deindustrialization should support programs to involve government as a broker between corporations and communities. The authors expressed fear that these types of progressive programs would be in jeopardy without such a policy.

Concerned primarily with the issue of community power, Fasenfest (1986) uses the case of the Central Industrial Park in Detroit to illustrate the power structures involved in local redevelopment policy. Fasenfest rejects pluralist and reformist notions of community power, defining power instead as "the ability to affect outcomes in one's favor over time" (109). Using this definition as a framework, Fasenfest seeks to understand how the decision to use eminent domain and tax abatements to build a new GM plant was made to look like it was the result of collective decision making at the community level. He argues that such a decision is often made, mistakenly, on the basis of cost-benefit analysis, which he argues has been shown to be an easily manipulated form of analysis (120). A more equitable analysis would "look beyond the resolution of particular issues confronting a given community, and look at the forces (local, national, and even international) which constrain both past outcomes and current possibilities" (121).

Utilizing the popular approach of comparing a region in the United States with a region in the United Kingdom, Beauregard, Lawless, and Detrick (1992) analyzed collaborative strategies for reindustrialization in Pittsburgh and Sheffield. Concerned more with the collaborative process of responding to deindustrialization rather than outcomes, the authors found that groups who advocated radical, labor-based policies to challenge the dominant consensus were often marginalized in the regional decision-making process. Moreover, the authors found that in both cases regional collaboration was not as regional or as consensual as one would hope and capital tended to flow unevenly within the collaborations (428). Overall, the authors concluded that, despite some variation in the collaborations seen in Sheffield and Pittsburgh, "what finally dominates one's perspective is a common involvement in a global capitalism that allows for only minor local variations" (428).

One of the few studies to specifically analyze growth regimes in Rust Belt cities is seen in Wilson and Wouters' (2004) article, "Spatiality and Growth Discourse: The Restructuring of America's Rust Belt Cities." The authors examine and probe the growth discourse by analyzing the experiences of three Rust Belt cities: St. Louis, Indianapolis, and Cleveland. Wilson and Wouters argue that "humanly created space has been neglected as a constructive ingredient" in the growth coalition discourse (124). Using content analysis and personal interviews, they find that growth coalitions in all three cities crafted discursive stories to convince the public of the enhanced city competition for resources and also to position the entrepreneurial developer as the "potential city salvationist" (135). Together, these two stories are interwoven to produce a coherent public message of growth as the ideal and provide little hope of a more progressive alternative. Referring to Soja's (1989) earlier research, Wilson and Wouters remind us that the public realm should still be seen as a politically neutral asset that can support either progressive or regressive political projects, depending on who informs the process. The authors end by identifying an important gap in the literature that is relevant to resilience studies of Midwestern regions as well. Specifically, they suggest that we do more to understand how these types of political projects muffle resistance and undermine oppositional discourses (136).

Together, the existing literature on growth coalitions and their involvement in urban redevelopment efforts tells us much about the relationship between communities, politics, and social theory in various post-industrial cities. What remains relatively untested as a concept, however, is the *region's* role within the framework of growth coalition theory. While city-level redevelopment efforts are important, they cannot address the ways in which regional prosperity or resilience is influenced by the politics that emanate from both inside and outside the city and the region. This gap in the literature suggests that there is value in research that attempts to address this very question.

The evolution of economic development

In the past, we have traditionally thought of economic development as wealth creation or economic growth. As such, the focus of economic development was largely on easily comprehensible measures like increasing the tax base and creating jobs. Today, however, economic development scholars provide comparatively broader and more inclusive ideas about economic development. Blakely and Green Leigh (2010) define local economic development as development that preserves and raises the community's standard of living through a process of human and physical infrastructure based on principles of equity and sustainability (75). Though most economic development scholars would agree in principle with Blakely and Green Leigh's definition, much debate still exists about what economic development is and what its goals should be (Koven and Lyons 2010). Our collective struggle to define economic development is emblematic of larger challenges seen within this field over the last half-century.

Unlike many other developed countries, economic development in the United States has historically been decentralized, meaning that much of the economic policy decisions is made at the state or local level. Economists often make the case for decentralization by arguing that it improves efficiency through the differentiation of local outputs, including infrastructure and capital, according to local needs (Oates 1972). It follows then that decentralized economic development that is sensitive to local strengths and shortcomings should be more effective in encouraging economic development than are centralized policies that treat all places as equal. Based on that argument, substantial powers thus exist at the subnational level, which has encouraged cutthroat competition between states and between municipalities seeking private industry.

At various points in the history of the United States, we have seen individual policies in support of national economic development goals; however, we have never had a formal economic development strategy at the national level. Any economic development interventions that have occurred at the national level have largely been through imprecise macroeconomic interventions in tax and spending policies (Eisinger 1988). What has resulted, then, is a national economy that is the sum of its subnational parts, all of which are constantly competing for investment and jobs. In addition to the challenges associated with an increasingly competitive subnational environment, metropolitan areas confronted three other important trends during the 1970s and 1980s that affected their adaptive resilience capabilities. These trends – increasing decentralization, shrinking federal resources, and international competition – all posed serious challenges for economic developers and leaders throughout the industrial Midwest.

While national leaders unsuccessfully struggled to formulate a federal economic development policy during the 1970s, economic development officials at the state and local levels dealt with the emergence of an increasingly deregulated, privatized, and free market-centered approach. The federal government began moving away from formalized economic development policy to such a degree that by the mid-1980s states and communities were developing their own smaller-scale industrial policies designed to focus on selected industries with a perceived comparative local advantage (Eisinger 1988, 6).

While state and local governments worked to identify their own economic development priorities, they did so under conditions of shrinking federal resources. Following decades of uninterrupted growth, intergovernmental aid from the federal government began to slow in 1978, forcing states to rethink their own funding priorities. After nearly three decades of growth in federal grant-in-aid to state and local governments, there was a 2.6 percent decrease in 1979 (ACIR 1986). Funding continued to slow considerably in the early 1980s as President Reagan's fiscally conservative policies took shape. The total number of federal intergovernmental transfer programs dropped from a high of 492 in 1978 to 405 in 1983. Aid programs as a percentage of total outlays from the federal government also dropped substantially during that time period, falling from 17 percent to 11.7 percent in just five years (Eisinger 1988, 69). Corresponding cutbacks in federal government funding for programs like Urban Development Actions Grants, Community Development Block Grants, and numerous Economic Development Administration grants also substantially impacted economic development at the local level.

In addition to these federal funding cutbacks and policy changes, regions also grappled with the stresses of increasing international trade and greater international access to the United States consumer market. Increased access resulted in increased imports, which provided more options at lower costs for US consumers but more competition for US producers. Increased international trade, perpetuated in part by US policymakers' indifference towards foreign competition in manufacturing, exposed weaknesses in many Midwestern economies. Once-dominant industries across the Midwest, many of which had long been bolstered by state and federal government efforts, began to realize that their failure to innovate had rendered large sectors of the economy inefficient, if not obsolete.

Economic development actors, processes, and tools

One of the ways that regions responded to these challenges was through the formalization of the economic development field. Today, economic development is a recognized profession, but that was not always the case. During the 1970s and 1980s, it was a burgeoning profession focused primarily on industrial recruitment and little else. Though economic development activities (by today's standards) were certainly taking place, economic developers largely did not yet exist.[1] Instead, we find that public sector officials partnering with private sector executives were the main catalysts for economic development during this period. Corporate recruiters, civic boosters, chambers of commerce, and business development agency representatives were also sometimes involved. Overall, there was much variation in terms of who was driving development decisions at the metropolitan level, which makes determining who was involved in the design and execution of these economic development interventions all the more difficult.

Research in planning and political science finds that decision-making power is generally held by the elites of the political, public, and economic realms and that the relative power of each depends in part on the region's governance and government structures, industrial composition, racial and class makeup and organization, as well as a confluence of state, national, and international forces (Mollenkopf 1983; Logan and Molotch 1987; Stone 1989; Imbroscio 1998; Davies 2002). As corporations belatedly scrambled to innovate, modernize, and invest in appropriate technologies during the 1970s and 1980s, local and regional leaders looked for ways to help corporations and to boost their economic bases. A growing uncertainty about federal support for economic development efforts led many state and local governments to find their own ways of addressing these problems (Kossy 1996). In many parts of the industrial Midwest, finding new solutions often meant searching for new sources of leadership and financial support. Rather than solely relying on federal grants for their economic development projects, regional leaders formed their own economic development organizations in order to set agendas, access scarce federal dollars, and leverage private investment for regional projects.

The growing importance of private investment for economic development brought with it an increase in the role of the private sector in the decision-making process (Cox and Mair 1988; Stone 1989). As private sector involvement grew, economic development and public officials became intermediaries who would act almost as regional cheerleaders, identifying potential projects and then negotiating deals to make them happen. Fittingly, the metrics during this period changed from ambiguous concepts like regional equity and poverty alleviation to employment rates and tax revenues (Kossy 1996).

During the 1980s, the tools used for economic development began to shift from federal and state entitlement programs to local and regional incentives, subsidies, business assistance, and the banking and development of land. In some regions, economic development officials set their sight on tourism by subsidizing the construction of amenities like stadiums, waterfronts, and other attractions.[2] Other economic development programs were focused on downtown living by either supporting or creating housing and amenities for people who wished to live downtown (McGovern 1998; Birch 2002). In most regions, however, economic development involved an amalgamation of policy and planning, driven largely by an increasingly powerful public and private sector elite.

Increased private sector involvement brought with it not only a change in the outcomes of the decision-making process but also a shift in the tone of the development agenda in most regions. As Kossy (1996) notes, "economic development was recast to address the whole constellation of issues affecting the business climate, as standards of community and industrial competitiveness became synonymous with community quality" (302). Recasting economic development meant something different for each region because the shape of each region's agenda was dependent upon who was involved in the process, the region's strengths and weaknesses, as well as its assets and constraints (Strange 1997; DiGaetano and Lawless 1999; de Socio 2007).

To help understand the importance of actors in the economic development process, let us envision, for a moment, the eight regions included in this study at the end of the 1970s. In each of these places, we can imagine diverse, lively, and contentious conversations centered on the question of how government and business leaders should respond to deindustrialization. The multitude of actors in each region most certainly presented a variety of opinions about how the strategy should unfold and whom it should involve. Making sense of this process is not an easy task. However, imagine that the creation of a regional strategy is similar to the preparation of a complex meal being made in a busy and over-staffed kitchen. This kitchen – like a microcosm of the region – is filled with many people making suggestions about how to prepare this meal. The suggestions they make are probably based on their own past experiences in making food and their own preferences about how they would like the meal to taste.

Whether or not their final suggestions will be taken into consideration will probably depend, in part, on: how loud their voice is; how experienced they are in making meals; how much their ingredients cost; and the perceived contribution that their suggested action or ingredient will make to the final product. We can imagine that if one of the more senior chefs gets her way, the meal might look a lot like the final product she had envisioned. Alternatively, if a group of the more junior chefs collectively come up with a more enticing option, we can see how their idea might greatly influence the final product. In the end, the meal could taste any number of different ways. The final recipe will likely depend on who is most convincing in their suggestions and who has the most power.[3]

Now, if we look at a region trying to devise a plan to deal with long-term industrial restructuring (their meal), we see that there are many different actors (chefs) who may wish to contribute to, or influence, the final plan. Similar to the chefs in the kitchen, regional actors will compete to have their suggestions heard. Some of the less powerful players – for example, the smaller municipalities – might band together to voice their desires. Alternatively, one major power broker – say, an executive of a large corporation or a suburban county executive – may simply demand that their suggestions be considered and maybe even implemented. The final regional response will then depend ultimately upon which regional actors are heard and which ideas they propose.[4] Making sense of these economic development responses and the various ways in which regions crafted their responses is the difficult task to which we now turn.

Typologizing economic development responses

When making comparisons across cases, researchers often utilize typologies as a way of categorizing, or sifting through, the various cases in a study. Though simple sorting does little in the way of explaining causality, typologies do make it easier to compare and contrast across cases as well as to identify commonalities worthy of future analysis. Typologies from a variety of disciplines abound (for more on economic development typologies, see Sternberg 1987, Peliserro and Fasenfest 1989, Reese 2006).[5] Numerous economic development scholars have grappled with the construction of typologies to assist in the categorization of local responses to restructuring. Despite their lack of standardization, typologies can be extremely useful in helping to tell a story about people, places, and actions for a given group or geography. In a discussion of clusters and industrial agglomerations, Martin and Sunley (2003) find that the classification and development of typologies is an important stage of theorizing and should be based on in-depth comparative analyses (13).

In their article, "Bowing Out, Bidding Down, and Betting on the Basics: Midwestern Responses to Deindustrialization in the 1980s", Markusen and Carlson (1988) described three main responses to economic restructuring. The first, which Markusen and Carlson call 'Bowing Out,' described instances in which economic development officials chose to cut their losses and abandon the idea of manufacturing reliance, focusing their economic development efforts instead on the attraction and growth of service sector employment opportunities. The second, 'Bidding Down,' involved strategies that tried to curtail manufacturing losses by decreasing the cost of doing business in a given region, enticing manufacturers either to move in or to stay by offering subsidies, tax credits, and other lucrative offers. The third, known as 'Betting on the Basics,' described economic development strategies that targeted existing heavy industry, emphasizing the retention and expansion of firms already in the area. Incidentally, it is this third category that Markusen and Carlson think most useful to industrial Midwestern regional economies. The authors argued that industrial retention, a hallmark of 'Betting on the Basics,' was the approach most concerned with community issues because it acknowledges the social cost of plant shutdowns. A fourth type of strategy, which I call 'Sharing the Wealth,' was later proposed by Clavel and Kleniewski (1990) and included strategies that embraced growth in the service sector and worked to incorporate linkage policies for the redistribution of related benefits in that sector.[6] To some extent, the 'Sharing the Wealth' approach embraced all three strategies – attraction, retention, and entrepreneurship – as long as there was an emphasis on equitable growth and linkage practices. The responses and corresponding strategies for the four response-types are summarized in Table 3.1.

Table 3.1 Markusen and Carlson's (1988) typology of responses and strategies to deindustrialization (summarized by author)

Response types	*Strategies*		
	Attracting business from elsewhere	*Fostering new business formation*	*Retaining local firms*
'Bowing Out': Concentrates resources on high tech, finance and service centers, Thurow's sunrise industries, and letting manufacturing die a natural death.	✓	✓	
'Bidding Down': Economy must revitalize its basic industry by overcoming uncompetitive cost structures (focuses on labor/management conflicts and on trimming the cost of doing business).	✓		✓
'Betting on the Basics': Advocates the targeting of existing heavy industry for ED efforts; rejects 'sunrise' industry route; emphasis on retention and expansion strategies.		✓	✓
'Sharing the Wealth': Focuses on service sector growth and the development of policies oriented toward labor and community groups rather than the corporate sector; incorporates linkages policies for the redistribution of service sector growth.	✓	✓	✓

In order to utilize this typology and to gain a diverse and robust understanding of each region's response, I drew upon qualitative data from various sources. Much of the data come from interviews I conducted with leaders from the public, private, and non-profit sectors, and leaders representing offices with urban, suburban, or regional interests. The interviewees were asked about the local effects of deindustrialization, the specific types of policies and programs implemented to address these effects, and the effectiveness of the chosen economic development strategies used in each region. Participants were also asked about their perception of their region's economy during the 1970s and 1980s, their responses to the economic changes that they saw unfolding, and their opinions on the efficacy of these responses.[7] They were also asked to discuss the local effects of deindustrialization, the specific types of policies and programs implemented to address these effects, and the effectiveness of the chosen economic development strategies they used. Each region was then categorized according to the response types described in Markusen and Carlson's typology.

In Chapters 5 and 6, each region will be analyzed using this typology to frame the discussion about economic development responses and adaptive resilience. Assigning regions to categories based on their economic development responses assists us as we look backwards in time. Although it falls short of proving causation, grouping cases by commonalities is a significant first step in understanding which types of policies were associated with 'good outcomes' and adaptive resilience and which were not.

Notes

1 During that time, there were two different organized groups for people working in the field of economic development: the American Economic Development Council (founded in 1926) and the Council for Urban Economic Development (founded in 1967). They later merged in 2001 to become the International Economic Development Council.

2 Scholars have long debated the efficacy of the amenity- and event-based attraction approaches to economic development (Gottlieb 1994; Burbank et al. 2002). In general, most of these subsidized projects, especially stadium construction, do not benefit the host region in the longer term (Bachelor 1998).

3 As political scientists and researchers of pluralism have long stated, power flows from a variety of different sources including those within the political realm and those outside of it (Jones and Bachelor 1993; Dahl 2005). Elite theorists have noted, however, that power is most often held by elites – from the public, private, and civic sectors – who generally have higher levels of resources and the backing of patrons (Putnam 1993).

4 Researchers of network density and social capital have found that dense networks of civic engagement create higher levels of trust, which in turn yields higher levels of cooperation in the face of a challenge (Putnam 1993). Within this communitarian approach, such cooperation is thought to reduce transaction costs and assist in collective action efforts, thereby increasing the likelihood of a desirable outcome (Putnam 2001). In slight contrast, the social mobilization literature suggests that acknowledgement of existing strategic relationships among various factions of interest within a community is necessary in order to then use these relationships as leverage in mobilizing collective actions (Skocpol 1996; DeFillipis 2001). Safford (2004) has argued that the combination and intersection of civic and economic relationships in a given area determines the degree to which its actors are able to facilitate collective action in response to deindustrialization.

5 Sternberg (1987) draws upon the tradition of political economy to group economic development strategies. Arguing that municipalities often have more economic development capabilities than they commonly use or even are aware of, Sternberg develops a helpful tool that outlines all that a state or local government can do to promote development. He ultimately proposes a typology of nine economic development policy groups that may prove useful to a practitioner who was unaware of existing tools or strategies for economic development. Peliserro and Fasenfest (1989) develop a simple typology of suburban economic development policy orientations. Although their work says nothing about inner cities or the broader region, it does offer some interesting findings for economic development policy orientations that could perhaps prove useful for either one of these other scales. They find that the economic development approaches of any given suburb generally could be assigned to one of five categories: aggressive, regulatory, cooperative, retentive, and reactive. Though their analysis makes no attempt to match these categories to any type of performance measure, the authors do make the helpful discovery that suburbs in the same metropolitan area contend with market forces, the strategic development policies of the central city and the surrounding suburbs. In a recent research note for *Economic Development Quarterly*, Reese (2006) uses cluster analysis to develop a typology of policy practice of cities, based on their local economic

development strategies. Her findings suggest that there are three main approaches to economic development. The first combines infrastructure investment and financial incentives. The second approach uses all possible techniques, including tax incentives, business assistance, and land development policies. The third approach is to remain passive and to do very little in the way of economic development.

6 In Clavel and Kleniewski's (1990) chapter, "Space for Progressive Local Policy: Examples from the US and the UK," the authors focus on the degree to which social control within a region affects the viability of certain responses. They make the case that national turmoil in the 1980s provided an "autonomy of the state" at the local level and encouraged local variation and experimentation within both the mainstream (pro-business) and progressive (pro-labor and community) political arenas (202). In laying out their argument, the authors build upon Markusen and Carlson's work to argue that a fourth category of local response should also be included, one that I call 'Sharing the Wealth' and that relates to strategies for the redistribution of service growth. Such an approach is similar to the 'Betting on the Basics' approach in that it necessitates a high degree of social control and is progressive in nature, but differs in that it focuses on the service industries instead of manufacturing. The contribution of such a distinction is useful in that it pinpoints the specific areas or industries in which the economic development strategies were to target. Like Markusen and Carlson, Clavel and Kleniewski provide examples for each of their categories but make no attempt to categorize regions at any broader scale.

7 Much of this interview process mirrored the process established in Mayer and Greenberg's (2001) study. The authors interviewed local leaders in 34 small- and medium-sized cities that experienced prolonged economic prosperity built around a major industry or firm and then underwent drastic economic decline when the industry or firm downsized or closed. The authors conducted extensive interviews with local officials, community leaders, and economic development practitioners, asking about their local responses. In the end, Mayer and Greenberg conclude that union issues and environmental undesirability were significant obstacles in many regions and that the most critical components of success in redevelopment efforts were leadership and community involvement (215).

References

Advisory Commission on Intergovernmental Relations (ACIR). 1986. *Significant Features on Fiscal Federalism, 1985–1986*. Washington, DC: Government Printing Office.

Bachelor, Lynn W. 1998. "Stadiums as Solution Sets: Baseball, Football and the Revival of Downtown Detroit." *Policy Studies Review* 15(1): 89–101.

Beauregard, Robert A., Paul Lawless, and Sabina Detrick. 1992. "Collaborative Strategies for Reindustrialization: Sheffield and Pittsburgh." *Economic Development Quarterly* 6(3): 418–430.

Birch, Eugenie Ladner. 2002. "Having a Longer View on Downtown Living." *Journal of the American Planning Association* 68 (1): 5–21.

Blakely, Edward J., and Nancey Green Leigh. 2010. *Planning Local Economic Development: Theory and Practice*. Thousand Oaks, CA: Sage.

Bluestone, Barry, and Bennett Harrison. 1982. *The Deindustrialization of America*. New York: Basic Books.

Burbank, Matthew J., Greg Andranovich, and Charles H. Heying. 2002. "Mega-Events, Urban Development, and Public Policy." *Review of Policy Research* 19(3): 179–202.

Clavel, Pierre, and Nancy Kleniewski. 1990. "Space for Progressive Local Policy: Examples from the U.S. and the U.K." In *Beyond the City Limits*, edited by John Logan and Todd Swanstrom, 199–236. Philadelphia: Temple University Press.

Cox, Kevin, and Andrew Mair. 1988. "Locality and Community in the Politics of Local Economic Development." *Annals of the Association of American Geographers* 78(2): 307–325.

Dahl, Robert. 2005. *Who Governs? Democracy and Power in an American City*. New Haven, CT: Yale University Press.

Davies, Jonathan S. 2002. "Urban Regime Theory: A Normative-empirical Critique." *Journal of Urban Affairs* 24(1): 1–17.

DeFillippis, James. 2001. "The Myth of Social Capital in Community Development." *Housing Policy Debate* 12(4): 781–806.

de Socio, Mark. 2007. "Business Community Structures and Urban Regimes: A Comparative Analysis." *Journal of Urban Affairs* 29(4): 339–366.

DiGaetano, A., and Klemanski, J. 1993. "Urban Regime Capacity: A Comparison of Birmingham, England and Detroit, Michigan." *Journal of Urban Affairs* 15(4): 367–384.

DiGaetano, Joe, and Paul Lawless. 1999. "Urban Governance and Industrial Decline: Governing Structures and Policy Agendas in Birmingham and Sheffield, England, and Detroit, Michigan, 1980–1997." *Urban Affairs Review* 34(4): 546–577.

Eisinger, Peter K. 1988. *The Rise of the Entrepreneurial State: State and Local Economic Development Policy in the United States*. Madison, WI: University of Wisconsin Press.

Fainstein, Norman, and Susan Fainstein, eds. 1983. *Restructuring the City: The Political Economy of Urban Development*. New York: Longman.

Fasenfest, David. 1986. "Community Politics and Urban Redevelopment: Poletown, Detroit and General Motors." *Urban Affairs Quarterly* 22(1): 101–123.

Feagin, Joe. 1988. *Free Enterprise City: Houston in Political-Economic Perspective*. New Brunswick, NJ: Rutgers University Press.

Gottdeiner, Mark. 1985. *The Social Production of Urban Space*. Austin, TX: The University of Texas Press.

Gottlieb, Paul D. 1994. "Amenities as an Economic Development Tool: Is there Enough Evidence?" *Economic Development Quarterly* 8(3): 270–285.

Horan, Cynthia, and Andrew E.G. Jonas. 1998. "Governing Massachusetts: Uneven Development and Politics in Metropolitan Boston." *Annals of the Association of American Geographers*, from the Annual Meeting of the Association of American Geographers, Boston, 83–95.

Imbroscio, David. 1998. "Reformulating Urban Regime Theory: The Division of Labor between State and Market Reconsidered." *Journal of Urban Affairs* 20(3): 233–248.

Jones, Bryan D., and Lynn W. Bachelor. 1993. *The Sustaining Hand: Community Leadership and Corporate Power*. Lawrence, KS: University Press of Kansas.

Judge, David, Gerry Stoker, and Harold Wolman, eds. 1995. *Theories of Urban Politics*. London, UK: Sage Publications.

Katznelson, Ira. 1981. *City Trenches*. Chicago, IL: The University of Chicago Press.

Kossy, Judith. 1996. "Economic Restructuring and the Restructuring of Economic Development Practice: A New York Perspective, 1985–1995." *Economic Development Quarterly* 10(4): 300–314.

Koven, Steven G., and Thomas S. Lyons. 2010. *Economic Development: Strategies for State and Local Practice*. Washington, DC: ICMA Press.

Logan, John R., and Harvey L. Molotch. 1987. *Urban Fortunes: The Political Economy of Place*. California: University of California Press.

Lord, George F. and Albert C. Price. 1992. "Growth Ideology in a Period of Decline: Deindustrialization and Restructuring, Flint Style." *Social Problems* 39(2): 155–169.

Markusen, Ann, and Virginia Carlson. 1988. "Bowing Out, Bidding Down, and Betting on the Basics: Midwestern Responses to Deindustrialization in the 1980s." Center for Urban Affairs and Policy Research, Working Paper, Northeastern University, Boston, MA.

Martin, R., & Sunley, P. (2003). "Deconstructing Clusters: Chaotic Concept or Policy Panacea?" *Journal of Economic Geography* 3(1): 5–35.

Mayer, Henry J., and Michael R. Greenberg. 2001. "Coming Back from Economic Despair: Case Studies of Small- and Medium-Size American Cities." *Economic Development Quarterly* 15(3): 203–216.

McGovern, Stephen J. 1998. *The Politics of Downtown Development*. Lexington, KY: University of Kentucky Press.

Mollenkopf, John. 1983. *The Contested City*. Princeton, NJ: Princeton University Press.

Molotch, Harvey. 1976. "The City as a Growth Machine." *American Journal of Sociology* 82: 309–332.

Molotch, Harvey. 1988. "Strategies and Constraints of Growth Elites." In *Business Elites and Urban Development*, edited by Scott Cummings, 25–48. Albany, NY: State University of New York Press.

Moore, Thomas A., and Gregory Squires. 1991. "Two Tales of a City: Economic Restructuring and Uneven Economic Development in a Former Company Town." *Journal of Urban Affairs* 13(2): 159–73.

Oates, Wallace. 1972. *Fiscal Federalism*. New York: Harcourt Brace Jovanovic.

Peliserro, John P., and David Fasenfest. 1989. "A Typology of Suburban Economic Development Policy Orientations." *Economic Development Quarterly* 3(4): 301–311.

Peterson, Paul. 1981. *City Limits*. Chicago, IL: University of Chicago Press.

Putnam, Robert D. 1993. *Making Democracy Work: Civic Traditions in Modern Italy*. Princeton, NJ: Princeton University Press.

Putnam, Robert D. 2001. "Community-based Social Capital and Educational Performance." In *Making Good Citizens: Education and Civil Society*, edited by Diane Ravitch and Joseph P. Viteritti, 58–95. New Haven, CT: Yale University Press.

Reese, Laura. 2006. "Do We Really Need Another Typology? Clusters of Local Economic Development Strategies." *Economic Development Quarterly* 20(4): 368–376.

Safford, Sean. 2009. *Why the Garden Club Couldn't Save Youngstown: The Transformation of the Rust Belt*. Cambridge, MA: Haward University Press.

Skocpol, Theda. 1996. "Unraveling from Above." *The American Prospect* 25 (Mar/Apr): 20–25.

Soja, E. W. 1989. *Postmodern Geographies: The Reassertion of Space in Critical Social Theory*. New York: Verso.

Sternberg, Ernest. 1987. "A Practitioner's Classification of Economic Development Policy Instruments, with Some Inspiration from Political Economy." *Economic Development Quarterly* 1(2): 149–161.

Stone, Clarence. 1989. *Regime Politics: Governing Atlanta, 1946–1988*. Lawrence, KS: University Press of Kansas.

Strange, Ian. 1997. "Directing the Show? Business Leaders, Local Partnership, and Economic Regeneration in Sheffield." *Environment and Planning C: Government and Policy* 15(1): 1–17.

Swanstrom, Todd. 1985. *The Crisis of Growth Politics: Cleveland, Kucinich, and the Challenge of Urban Populism*. Philadelphia: Temple University Press.

Wilson, David and Jared Wouters. 2004. "Spatiality and Growth Discourse: The Restructuring of America's Rust Belt Cities." *Journal of Urban Affairs* 25 (2): 123–138.

4 Eight regions changing

Researchers have long been cognizant of that fact that you cannot paint a picture of an area as large as the United States Rust Belt with just one broad stroke; doing so overlooks the many intricacies seen in a region this large and diverse. To be certain, there are a variety of uniting features that make the region a cohesive unit. Most of the Rust Belt is known for being in the heartland and near or on one of the Great Lakes, and for having strong agricultural associations and long-standing ties to heavy industry. Yet, in spite of such important commonalities, the Rust Belt region is a surprisingly nuanced and complicated place. The Rust Belt includes more than 100 metropolitan areas, and nine major metropolitan regions and parts of eight different states.[1] Each city has its own proclivities, each region its own disposition, and each state has its own political flavor, making it exceedingly complicated to understand the Rust Belt region and the parts that comprise it.

In order to uncover the complexities of the Rust Belt and its various interlocking parts, a deeper and more thorough investigation is necessary. In this chapter, I present a brief introduction to these regions and their common characteristics. In Chapters 5 and 6, the eight case studies are presented and grouped according to the type of economic development response they employed. Before we analyze the responses seen in these eight regions, however, we must first understand the unique economics, politics, and demography of each individual region. Since this is a story of regions transitioning from manufacturing, the eight regions will be presented in order from most dependent on manufacturing to least dependent on manufacturing, as measured by their manufacturing employment levels in 1970.[2] A general discussion of each region will be provided first, followed at the end of the chapter by a preliminary discussion of commonalities across cases and then a discussion of metrics to assess adaptive resilience and 'good outcomes.'

Eight distinct metropolitan regions

No two Rust Belt regions are alike. Though similarities may exist in some instances, each of the following regions differs greatly in terms of size, political

Table 4.1 Regions by manufacturing dependence and sector (1970)

Region	*Manufacturing as percent of total employment (1970)*	*Sectoral strengths in the 1970s*
Detroit	31.6	Automobiles, transportation equipment
Milwaukee	31.4	Machine manufacturing, industrial controls
Cleveland	31.2	Primary metals, machine manufacturing, transportation equipment
Buffalo	29.9	Steel, automobile parts
Cincinnati	28.3	Consumer goods, machine manufacturing, transportation equipment
Pittsburgh	27.5	Steel, glass, aluminum
Indianapolis	24.2	Consumer electronics, industrial automation and instrumentation
Columbus	22.2	Machine manufacturing, fabricated metals, food processing

Source: U.S. Department of Commerce, Bureau of Economic Analysis – REIS.

leanings, leadership base, assets, and constraints. Understanding how these regions differ in these and other ways is an important precondition for determining how they responded to the challenge of deindustrialization. As Table 4.1 attests, the eight regions included in this study varied substantially in terms of their dependence on manufacturing in general and within various key subsectors. We begin with a brief discussion of Detroit, the most dependent on manufacturing of all eight regions.

The metropolitan statistical area (MSA) of Detroit-Warren-Livonia includes the six counties of Lapeer, Livingston, Macomb, Oakland, St. Clair, and Wayne. In 2012, the region was America's eleventh-largest and was home to 4.3 million people. Though these numbers have varied little since 2000, fluctuations during the previous century caused turbulent changes in Detroit's population and its employment base. The region saw population losses in both the 1970s and the 1980s. The regional economy has long been dependent on automobile manufacturing and is home to the 'Big Three' automobile manufacturers: Chrysler, Ford, and General Motors. Though much has changed in recent years as these companies have modified both the techniques and locations of their production processes, Detroit remains an important location for both automobile manufacturing and related support businesses such as parts, electronics, and design suppliers (Klier and McMillen 2005).

The Milwaukee-Waukesha-West Allis MSA was home to 1.56 million people in 2012 and consists of four counties: Milwaukee, Waukesha, Washington, and Ozaukee. The region runs along the western border of Lake Michigan and includes the confluence of the Menomonee, Kinnickinnic, and Milwaukee Rivers. Like so many of the other regions in this study, the Milwaukee region was originally settled because of its strategic location. Long known for its brewing and manufacturing, the region has faced substantial difficulty in the wake of deindustrialization but still remains a manufacturing-intensive economy. Early strengths in tool making contributed to the region's specialization in machine manufacturing and industrial controls during the 1970s and 1980s. Population has remained relatively stable in the region, although it did see a slight decrease during the 1970s.

The Cleveland-Elyria-Mentor MSA had a population of 2.1 million people and was the 26th largest MSA in 2012. The region consists of five counties: Cuyahoga, Geauga, Lake, Lorain, and Medina. During the early twentieth century, Cleveland rose to prominence as a center of industry, particularly in steel manufacturing. The region's early success was due in part to its strategic location on the Cuyahoga River and Lake Erie, which helped to establish the city as an important manufacturing hub. Anchor industries during the 1970s and 1980s included primary metals, fabricated metals, non-electrical and electrical machinery, and transportation equipment. Population within the region decreased significantly during the 1970s and 1980s, but it has since begun to stabilize during the 1990s and 2000–10s.

The Buffalo-Niagara Falls MSA is a moderately sized metropolitan region, of approximately 1.1 million people in 2012. The region consists of two counties: Erie and Niagara, which are home to the cities of Buffalo and Niagara Falls, respectively. At the dawn of the twentieth century, Buffalo emerged as an important location for grain storage, steel production, railroad and shipping commerce, automobile production, and aerospace design and construction. As the original western terminus of the Erie Canal System, the region also saw substantial benefits from commerce associated with Great Lakes trade and transportation. These industrial and locational strengths, as well as inexpensive and plentiful hydroelectric power from the Niagara River, afforded the Buffalo region continued success throughout the first half of the twentieth century. Employment losses in the steel industry, a significant part of the region's economic base during the 1970s and 1980s, however, irrevocably harmed the region's economy in ways that can still be seen today.

The Cincinnati-Middletown MSA is a 15-county region spanning portions of the states of Indiana, Ohio, and Kentucky. The region was home to approximately 2.1 million people in 2012. Industrial development within the region began during the second half of the nineteenth century. Much of this development benefited greatly from the strong transportation links afforded by the Miami and Erie Canal, a canal that was completed in 1845 and connected the region to Lake Erie. The canal, and later the railroads, gave Cincinnati a locational advantage in terms of shipping and transportation and also helped the region gain access to valuable raw materials. These two advantages, combined with a strong local demand for goods and a strong and skilled local workforce, helped the Cincinnati economy to gain ground throughout much of the nineteenth and twentieth centuries. Industrial strengths during the 1970s and 1980s included manufacturing of consumer goods, machinery, and transportation equipment. The region has since shifted away from heavy manufacturing and moved towards chemical and pharmaceutical goods, as well as financial services.

The Pittsburgh MSA was home to approximately 2.4 million people in 2012 and consists of seven counties: Allegheny, Armstrong, Beaver, Butler, Fayette, Washington, and Westmoreland. Allegheny County, where the City of Pittsburgh is located, has long been considered the center of the region both politically and economically (Killikenny 1906). The Pittsburgh region as a whole emerged as an industrial center based on its high-grade coal reserves in the mid-nineteenth century, and its dominance in the steel manufacturing sector grew throughout the early twentieth century (Clark 1989). By the late 1970s and early 1980s, job losses in manufacturing, many within the steel industry, were cause for great concern in the Pittsburgh region. Between 1980 and 1986, the region lost 115,000 manufacturing jobs, with nearly 50 percent of these losses coming from the steel industry alone. The severity of this loss was somewhat masked by the relative gains seen in other, non-manufacturing sectors, specifically in healthcare, education, technology, and financial services (Detrick 1999). Overall, total regional employment decreased by 7 percent during this time period as Pittsburgh moved from a production economy to a service economy.

The Indianapolis-Carmel MSA is a nine-county region, of approximately 1.9 million people in 2012. In the early- to mid-twentieth century, this state capital's economy largely revolved around government and heavy industry, including the manufacturing of pharmaceuticals and durable goods like motor vehicle parts and machine tools. Having consciously moved away from most of its manufacturing in the late twentieth century, the Indianapolis economy today is more diverse, with specialties in healthcare, education, finance, and education. Another major economic engine for the region is tourism, and specifically tourism related to sports and conventions.

The Columbus region was home to 1.9 million people in 2012. The metropolitan area includes eight counties and is the third-largest MSA in Ohio, behind Cleveland and Cincinnati. Earlier manufacturing strengths include an emphasis on machinery, fabricated metal, and food processing, which to some extent remain a small but important part of the region's economy today. As Ohio's state capital, the region's economy is largely dominated by the public sector, including state and local government employees as well as employees working for the Ohio State University. In 2012, there were approximately 146,000 local and state government employees, about 15 percent of all employees working in the region (Bureau of Labor Statistics). Beyond a strong public sector, the region also has a very strong financial services sector – including numerous insurance and banking corporations – and a strong clothing retail base that has grown considerably in the last few decades.

Mapping common traits and characteristics

Looking back at Table 4.1 and at the descriptions provided above, we can begin making some preliminary observations about these regions. First, Table 4.1 shows that there is not a huge difference in manufacturing dependence between the most dependent region, Detroit (31.6 percent), and the sixth-ranked region, Pittsburgh (27.5 percent). While there is a natural breaking point between Pittsburgh and Indianapolis, all of the regions that were at least as dependent as Pittsburgh – meaning a dependence on manufacturing of 27.5 percent or more – experienced pretty similar difficulties during the 1970s and 1980s. Most of these regions saw substantial job losses in manufacturing, extensive fiscal challenges, and population stagnation or decline. Indianapolis and Columbus, on the other hand, which were comparatively less dependent on manufacturing, suffered considerably less during this deindustrialization period.

One other thing we learn from these brief introductions is that among the more popular specializations were the manufacturing of steel, automobiles, and other transportation equipment. Steel towns tended to fall in the middle of the spectrum, with a dependence on manufacturing of around 27 to 29 percent. Automobiles and transportation equipment were seen in Detroit, the most dependent, and in Cleveland and Cincinnati, which both exhibited mid-range manufacturing dependency. Higher-technology types of industrial strengths tended to be seen in regions on the lower end of the manufacturing-dependency spectrum, most notably in Indianapolis, and to some extent in Columbus.

A simple listing of industrial strengths tells us only about the composition of each region's economic base, but when we map these strengths against more detailed information about the size of these industries over time, this information becomes inherently more useful. Figure 4.1 depicts changes in the size of these manufacturing subsectors in the United States from 1969 to 2003. Featured in this chart are the main industrial strengths of the eight case study regions. Mapping the changes in each subsector over time adds a temporal dimension to our discussion of economic change.

Because different sectors were affected by deindustrialization in different ways and at different times, we can imagine that each region, depending on its particular specializations, would experience deindustrialization differently. For instance, the earliest warning signs of industrial decline occurred in transportation equipment and primary metals, both of which saw little recovery during the late 1970s and early 1980s. One would expect, then, that regions that depended on these sectors for their livelihoods may have reacted earlier than regions where other less-affected or later-affected industries were dominant. In the case of transportation equipment, we might expect to see earlier responses from Detroit, Cleveland, and Cincinnati. Or, in the case of

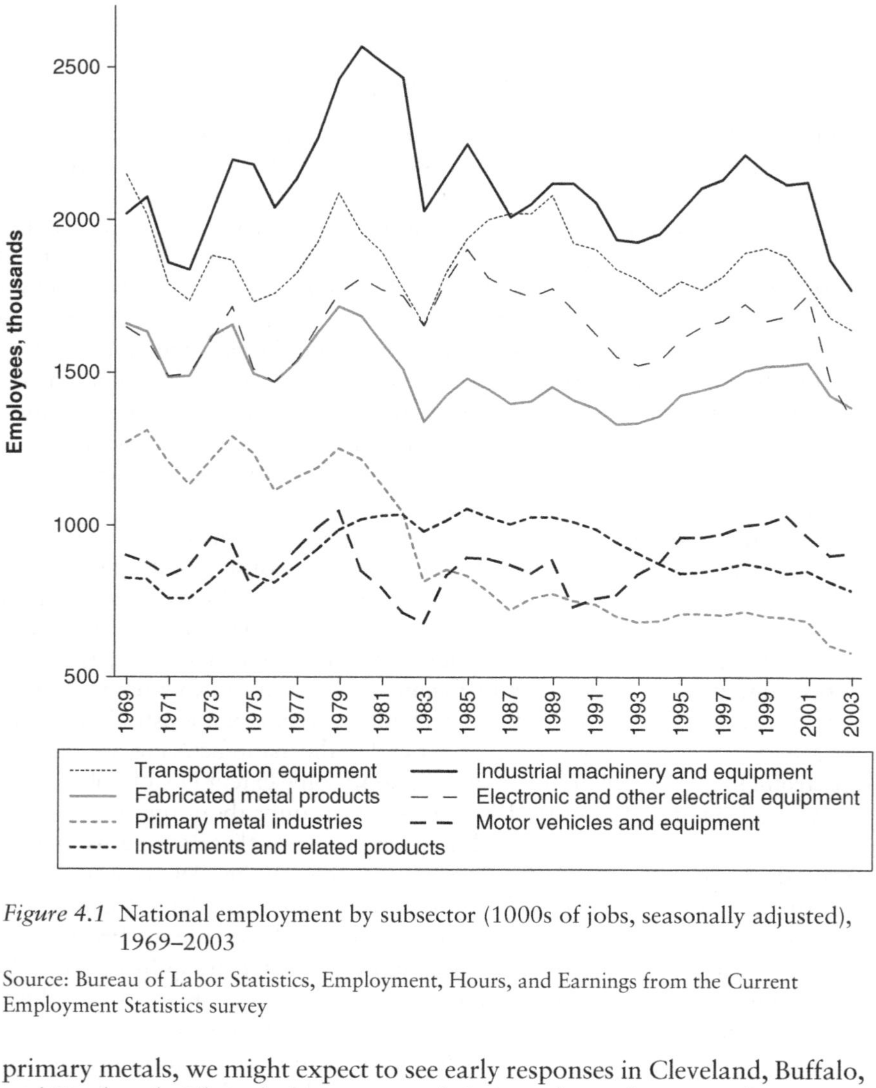

Figure 4.1 National employment by subsector (1000s of jobs, seasonally adjusted), 1969–2003

Source: Bureau of Labor Statistics, Employment, Hours, and Earnings from the Current Employment Statistics survey

primary metals, we might expect to see early responses in Cleveland, Buffalo, and Pittsburgh. Though the nature and timing of specific regional responses will be discussed later on, it is useful here to begin thinking about the unique experiences of each of the eight case study regions. To that end, we continue exploring quantitative measures of these regions below.

Adaptive resilience: response and recovery

Now that we know some of the important compositional characteristics of these eight regions, it seems useful to begin looking at how these regions fared, quantitatively, vis-à-vis some simple measures of resilience and hypothetical 'good outcomes.' In her case study of Buffalo, Foster (2006) proposed two main ways of looking at adaptive resilience in light of slow-burning crises like deindustrialization. Foster differentiates between response and recovery resilience, asking how a region responded to a given challenge and how well it recovered from that challenge over time. For the Buffalo case study, Foster presented a number of standard measures for two separate time periods. First, she examined figures from the 1970s and 1980s to determine how well the region responded to deindustrialization. Next, she examined figures from 1989 to 2000 to determine how well the region performed in the recovery phase. To gauge the region's relative performance, figures for Buffalo were compared to other regions in the state of New York as well as other regions of similar size and industrial composition. Ultimately, she concluded that both Buffalo's response resilience and recovery resilience were comparatively low, which would suggest a lack of 'good outcomes' for the region. Below, I borrow from this framework to conduct an initial quantitative assessment of the eight case study regions.

Table 4.2 summarizes the performance of the eight case study regions using Foster's (2006) measures of *response* resilience, namely in terms of population change, employment change, per capita income, and poverty in the 1970s and 1980s. In order to gauge each region's relative performance, the mean for all eight regions is also provided. Those regions that performed worse than the mean for the group on any given measure are marked in bold. Among the more obvious observations seen in Table 4.2 is the correlation between manufacturing dependence and below-average performance across most indicators. Regions in the top half (meaning most dependent on manufacturing) are more likely to fall below the mean than those regions found in the bottom half. Detroit, the most dependent on manufacturing, was below the mean on every indicator except per capita income, which implies that if you were lucky enough to have a job, your income was probably above average. Milwaukee, just behind Detroit in manufacturing dependence, was below average across many measures; notable exceptions include major employment growth between 1969 and 1979, as well as modest population growth between 1979 and 1989. Among the more manufacturing-dependent regions, Milwaukee performed slightly better than expected. Despite being below the mean on many measures, the Milwaukee region did see population growth in the second half of the response period and modest growth in employment in both portions of the response period. Indicators for Cleveland and Buffalo paint a pretty dismal picture; Buffalo fell below the average across all measures except poverty, while Cleveland fell below on all but per capita income and poverty. Again, these findings suggest that there was little, at least quantitatively, to suggest the presence of adaptive resilience or 'good outcomes' in these regions.

Like Detroit, the Cleveland per capita income measure suggests that remaining jobs paid pretty well in the region. In Cincinnati, the opposite

Table 4.2 Selected characteristics of eight case study regions in the response period (1969–1989)

Region	*Manufacturing as percent of total employment (1970)*	*Percent population change*		*Percent employment change*		*Per capita income*		*Poverty*			
		1969–1979	*1979–1989*	*1969–1979*	*1979–1989*	*1989 ($)*	*Percent change 1969–1989*	*Rate (1970)*	*Rate (1990)*	*Central city to suburbs ratio (1970)*	*Central city to suburbs ratio (1990)*
Detroit	**31.6**	**–0.7**	**–2.4**	**9.7**	**7.9**	$15,649	**35.0**	8.4	**13.0**	**2.2**	2.4
Milwaukee	**31.4**	**–0.4**	2.5	20.6	**6.2**	$14,785	**34.6**	7.8	11.6	1	**7.1**
Cleveland	**31.2**	**–6.5**	**–3.1**	**6.2**	**0.8**	$15,092	**31.6**	8.8	**11.8**	1.6	1.6
Buffalo	**29.9**	**–7.9**	**–4.3**	**3.8**	**5.1**	**$13,403**	**33.3**	9.0	**12.0**	**2.4**	**2.6**
Cincinnati	28.3	9.5	5.1	18	16.8	**$14,401**	42.6	**10.7**	11.5	**2.0**	0.8
Pittsburgh	27.5	10.3	**–6.8**	**8.2**	**–0.6**	**$13,785**	39.1	**10.1**	**12.1**	**4.3**	0.3
Indianapolis	24.2	9	7.1	18.9	18.3	$14,936	40.1	8.6	9.5	0.1	**3.1**
Columbus	22.2	38.5	10.7	27.8	21.4	**$14,537**	43.5	**10.3**	**11.8**	0.7	2.1
Mean	28.3	**6.5**	**1.1**	**14.2**	9.5	**$14,574**	37.5	**9.2**	**11.7**	**1.8**	**2.5**

Source: Building Resilient Regions database.

Note: Mean denotes average value for the eight case study regions. The regions that performed worse than the mean for the group on any given measure are marked in bold.

was true – it did surprisingly well, performing above average on all measures *except* per capita income. Therefore, the kinds of jobs that were in Cincinnati, although comparatively stable, probably did not pay as well as in other Rust Belt regions. Below-average per capita income was also apparent in Pittsburgh, as was population decline in the second half of the response period and employment throughout. In these regions, there were some but not many 'good outcomes,' which suggests that these regions had mixed results in their navigation of the deindustrialization challenge.

Two regions that exhibited greater success in navigating the trials of deindustrialization were Indianapolis and Columbus. Quantitatively, both regions fared much better than their counterparts, displaying above-average scores across all indicators except for below-average per capita income and above-average poverty in Columbus.

Overall, these relatively simple indicators of response resilience suggest that manufacturing dependence likely did matter. Regions where manufacturing dependence was pronounced generally performed poorly on most of Foster's (2006) key response indicators and did not produce many 'good outcomes.' It follows, then, that the degree to which your economy was rooted in manufacturing likely played an important role in how much response resilience you exhibited and how well you navigated the adaptive resilience cycle. However, aberrations certainly abound. The relatively solid performance of Cincinnati, which basically started with average manufacturing dependence, encourages additional explanation. Pittsburgh, with its relatively low manufacturing dependence, performed surprisingly low on measures of population, employment, and per capita income. Further explanation of these and other remaining questions about regional responses to deindustrialization will be explored in the remainder of the book.

Shifting gears, Table 4.3 summarizes elements of regional resilience for the *recovery* period, or the 1990s decade, which followed two decades of decline. Again, quantitative indicators for various measures across all eight regions are presented. The goal for this post-deindustrialization assessment is to identify those regions that performed well on various standard economic indicators, determine the extent to which each region experienced 'good outcomes' in the recovery period, and raise questions for the remaining analysis.

The findings from Table 4.3 suggest that manufacturing dependence within the eight regions decreased dramatically since 1970 but the overall rank of each region in that regard remained largely unchanged. This continuity in ranking suggests that, even though manufacturing contracted across the board, it still mattered most in the regions where it had always had a strong presence. More importantly, it also hints at the possibility that a manufacturing legacy is generally a strong legacy and one that is perhaps quite difficult to move away from. A more thorough discussion of the challenges associated with a manufacturing legacy is provided in subsequent chapters.

Another important conclusion that can be drawn from Table 4.3 is that many of those same underperformers from the response period remained

Table 4.3 Selected characteristics of eight case study regions in the recovery period (1989–2000)

Region	*Manufacturing as percent of total employment (2000)*	*Percent population change*		*Per capita income*		*Poverty*	
		1989–2000	*1989–2000*	*2000 ($)*	*Percent change 1989–2000*	*Rate (2000)*	*Central city to suburbs ratio (2000)*
Detroit	**18.1**	**4.8**	**15.3**	$24,275	15.8	**10.6**	1.9
Milwaukee	**17.5**	**4.8**	**15.6**	$23,003	16.2	**10.4**	**5.3**
Cleveland	**15.9**	**2.2**	**12.2**	**$22,319**	**10.4**	**10.6**	1.4
Buffalo	13.6	**−1.6**	**3.0**	**$20,143**	**12.2**	**11.9**	**2.4**
Cincinnati	13.5	8.9	24.1	$22,947	19	9.5	0.7
Pittsburgh	10.4	**−1.5**	**12.5**	**$20,935**	**13.4**	**10.8**	0.3
Indianapolis	11.8	17.8	30.6	$23,198	16	8.6	**2.7**
Columbus	9.9	14.8	29.4	$23,020	18.2	10.1	**2.1**
Mean	**13.7**	**6.8**	**17.8**	**$22,713**	**14.6**	**10.3**	**2.1**

Source: Building Resilient Regions database.

Note: Mean denotes average value for the eight case study regions. The regions that performed worse than the mean for the group on any given measure are marked in bold.

below average in the recovery period as well. Detroit, Milwaukee, Cleveland, and Buffalo remained relatively consistent underperformers across most of these resilience measures, suggesting a lack of 'good outcomes' in these places. Cincinnati continued to walk the middle ground, and Pittsburgh underperformed on most measures, despite a much lower manufacturing dependence than the other underperformers. Some of the interesting changes seen between response and recovery were double-digit population growth in Indianapolis and Columbus and exceedingly high employment growth in Cincinnati and Indianapolis. Also, somewhat surprisingly, Milwaukee, Cincinnati, and Columbus all saw their per capita income standings shift from below the mean to above it during this time period.

All of these shifts – for better or worse – suggest that fortunes may have changed for some of these regions between the response and recovery periods. Changing fortunes beg the question of whether or not these shifts had anything to do with the individual region's response or whether it was purely luck that changed certain regional outcomes. As was also true in Foster's case study of Buffalo, we are left with many questions about the adaptive resilience of regions. Namely, we must consider the specific responses crafted in each of these regions, the efficacy of those responses in the long run, and the relationship between these responses and 'good outcomes.' We must also ask about the resources available in each region to help with the response and subsequent recovery. Even more importantly, we must ask who was responsible for crafting these responses, what were their intentions, and how did they decide upon their response.

Answering these questions requires additional qualitative data generally gleaned from interviews with actors and consultation of planning documents in these regions, which is the focus of Chapters 5 and 6. Before we begin down that path, however, let us revisit the research questions posed in the Introduction. Armed now with a preliminary understanding of deindustrialization, adaptive resilience, and economic development, I propose three related hypotheses to guide our study of the relationships between local economic development responses and adaptive resilience in deindustrializing regions. Recall that the first question asks about the actors involved in each region's decision-making process. The second asks about the motivations and goals of each region in crafting their response. The issue of adaptive resilience, and the extent to which it was observed in each region, is the focus of the third research question. The hypotheses described below will guide us during the qualitative explorations that follow in Chapters 5 and 6.

Economic development decisions, which are often quite costly and sometimes rather risky, ought not to be made unilaterally, nor made in a vacuum. Instead, they ideally involve a host of actors (recall the many chefs in the kitchen example) who represent an array of interests. The optimal number and variety of actors is not known, but one can readily imagine that there are benefits to diversity and a multiplicity of perspectives, especially in regions that are confronting a serious challenge like deindustrialization. Such variety and insight would likely contribute to a more flexible and reflective response. It seems reasonable, then, that *regions with a diverse and broadly representative decision-making body would be more likely to exhibit adaptive resilience and experience 'good outcomes.'* We would expect such regions to turn the metaphorical 'corner' by bringing together a diverse coalition of economic development actors to help navigate the economic uncertainties associated with deindustrialization. Alternatively, we might expect to see less evidence of adaptive resilience in places where unilateral decisions were made or in places where one sector of leadership wielded the majority of the decision-making power.

Second, if we think about the ongoing and very public challenges seen in manufacturing-dependent places like Detroit and Cleveland – regions that have been relatively forthcoming in their commitment to manufacturing and ostensibly to 'Betting on the Basics' – we cannot help but notice the substantial economic challenges these regions have experienced in recent years. It seems plausible, then, that *regions in which leaders committed to manufacturing by 'Betting on the Basics' will not adapt as readily or as well as regions where leaders pursued other alternatives.* If this holds true, we should expect to see Detroit and other regions that 'Bet on the Basics' respond poorly to the challenges of deindustrialization and exhibit little adaptive resilience. By the same token, adaptive resilience should be more readily observed in places that emphasized economic diversification, flexibility, and creativity in their economic development responses. Therefore, we would expect to see comparatively greater adaptive resilience in places that 'Bowed Out,' 'Bid Down,' or 'Shared the Wealth.'

A third hypothesis stems from the old adage that 'the early bird gets the worm.' More specifically, it seems plausible that *adaptive resilience will be seen in regions where leaders responded to early signs of deindustrialization and quickly developed an appropriate economic development response.* We would expect such regions to move fairly quickly to turn the metaphorical 'corner' by navigating the collapse and uncertainty associated with the release phase. Alternatively, we might expect to see less evidence of adaptive resilience in places where leaders reacted slowly to the realities of deindustrialization. In such cases, we might also expect to see a more reactive, rather than proactive, approach to the crafting of a response and a lengthy conservation or release phase. It makes sense that regional leaders who worked to get out ahead of the manufacturing downturn would exhibit more adaptive resilience than regional leaders who denied the existence of deindustrialization or ignored calls to respond.

Armed with these hypotheses and important research questions, further exploration of these regions and the economic development responses they developed in the wake of deindustrialization will follow in the rest of the book. The next two chapters will marry what we now know, quantitatively, about the responses and recoveries seen in these regions with a series of qualitative accounts of what happened in each. Together, these findings will help us to better understand adaptive resilience in the context of these eight regions.

Notes

1 The Chicago Metropolitan region is the ninth, and largest, region in the Rust Belt. It has been excluded from this study, however, because its economy, size, and recovery differ so greatly from the other eight regions.
2 The starting point of 1970 has been chosen because, for many of these regions, the early 1970s marked the peak of their manufacturing employment base.

References

Bureau of Labor Statistics, U.S. Department of Labor. *Current Employment Statistics* Accessed March 16, 2014. www.bls.gov/ces/.

Clark, Gordon. 1989. "Pittsburgh in Transition: Consolidation of Prosperity in an Era of Economic Restructuring." In *Economic Restructuring and Political Response,* edited by Robert Beauregard, 41–69. Newbury Park: Sage Press.

Detrick, Sabina. 1999. "The Post Industrial Revitalization of Pittsburgh: Myths and Evidence." *Journal of Planning Literature* 34(1): 4–12.

Foster, Kathryn. 2006. "A Case Study Approach to Understanding Regional Resilience." Working Paper 2007–08. University of California (November).

Killikenny, Sarah Hutchens. 1906. *The History of Pittsburgh: Its Rise and Progress.* Pittsburgh, PA: B.C. and Gordon Montgomery.

Klier, Thomas and Daniel P. McMillen. 2005. "Clustering of Auto Supplier Plants in the U.S.: GMM Spatial Logit for Large Samples." Working Paper, Federal Reserve Bank of Chicago, WP 2005–18.

5 The 'Basic Betters'

Detroit, Milwaukee, Cleveland, and Buffalo

A common response to the challenges of deindustrialization was for regions to struggle against change, ignore calls for diversification, and attempt to recreate the economic base of the past. In this chapter, the focus is on four regions that chose to do just that – 'Bet on the Basics.' During the 1970s and 1980s, Detroit, Milwaukee, Cleveland, and Buffalo all crafted strategies that focused primarily on the retention and expansion of manufacturing firms, and most struggled to adapt as a result. Unsurprisingly, the response seen in Detroit most closely followed this approach.

Given that Detroit's economy was so intertwined and so dependent on a manufacturing base that had done so well for so long, one can understand why regional leaders there may have considered themselves immune to deindustrialization. This sense of immunity, combined with a reliance on practices that had worked well in the past, led leaders in Detroit to 'Bet on the Basics.' Recall from Chapter 3 that 'Betting on the Basics' describes regional responses focused on existing heavy industry, emphasizing industrial retention and the expansion of firms already in the area; all of which collectively helped to solidify the region's position within the conservation phase.

Outside of Detroit, the economies of other Rust Belt regions were slightly less specialized or dependent on one given sector of the economy or any one particular product or corporation. To some extent, these other regions had options and were probably less inclined to commit to any predisposed trajectory. Though it would not have been easy, regional leaders in Milwaukee, Cleveland, and Buffalo could have focused on something other than industrial retention and expansion. Nevertheless, all four of these regions chose a similar approach, despite appearing to have other options.

An analysis of the processes by which all four regions arrived at their own responses, as well as a discussion of related outcomes, follows below. A comparable analysis for the remaining four regions, all of which opted to pursue other types of economic development responses, follows in Chapter 6. In both chapters, commonalities across these case study regions are identified and a series of lessons from both the data collected as well as subsequent analysis are offered. This chapter begins by briefly introducing the regions, their economies, and the processes by which they crafted their response. Regions are presented in order from most dependent on manufacturing to least dependent as measured by manufacturing as a percent of total employment in 1970. We begin first with the Detroit region.

Detroit

As the home to the 'Big Three' automobile manufacturers (Chrysler, Ford, and General Motors), Detroit's regional economy has long been dependent on automobile manufacturing. Because of its higher concentration of automobile manufacturing and supporting industries, changes in the economy that affected the broader automobile industry disproportionately affected the Detroit region (Ingrassia and White 1995). The extent to which the Detroit region relied on the automobile industry became increasingly clear during the 1970s. Despite warning signs in the past, the recession of 1969–1970 and the energy crisis of 1973 significantly impacted the Detroit region. A sharp drop in demand for large American cars, coupled with the rise of foreign automobiles, meant that Detroit's automobile industry had to innovate or make significant changes in order to stay competitive.

In search of lower costs and higher-quality products, many automakers either introduced labor-saving technologies to their production facilities or moved production facilities to other, lower-cost regions, both of which generally resulted in significant job losses for the Detroit region. Between 1950 and 1970, Detroit's share of national automotive employment decreased from 35 to 20 percent, as corporations looked to other, less expensive parts of the country and the world for their production facilities. The integration of automation technologies continued through the 1980s and 1990s, generally increasing productivity and efficiency, while simultaneously causing record-high outputs of motor vehicles and a widespread reduction in the number of automobile workers needed (Farley et al. 2000).

In Detroit, three main groups of actors made decisions about how to respond to deindustrialization: politicians, including city, suburban, and regional officials; leaders from the private sector; and labor leaders. As one might expect, politicians were among the most vocal groups involved in the decision-making process. Among the politicians, one of the primary players was Detroit's Mayor Coleman Young (1973–1994), under which a "corporatist governing structure was forged around the city's downtown renaissance agenda" (DiGaetano and Lawless 1999, 559). To that end, Young did have a series of successes, including the creation of the Detroit Economic Growth Corporation, Downtown Development Authority, Economic Development Corporation, and various built projects (Bachelor 1998). Other important political voices of this period included Governors William Milliken (1969–1983), a moderate Republican, and his successor, James Blanchard (1983–1991), a Democrat. Despite their opposing political viewpoints, both Blanchard and Milliken were seen as persons sympathetic to automobile corporation interests, who would do anything in their power to keep these corporations in Michigan, and mainly in the Detroit region.

Suburban officials, who were more likely to be Republican, were also important members of the decision-making process. One of the main Republican voices in Oakland County is the long-standing County Executive L. Brooks Patterson, who has been an outspoken advocate for suburban development. Among government agencies, regional representation came from the Southeastern Michigan Council of Governments (SEMCOG), a membership organization of local governments in Livingston, Macomb, Monroe, Oakland, St. Clair, Washtenaw, and Wayne Counties.

The Detroit Regional Chamber is the main regional business organization and one of the largest and most powerful chambers of commerce in the country. The Chamber, along with another business group, Detroit Renaissance, generally represented the white, corporate elite interests (Jo 2002). Other business-led groups, like the Detroit Economic Growth Corporation and New Detroit, which were designed by Mayor Young and his supporters, were called "a forum for articulating the black agenda" (Rich 1989, 81). Given the pro-business orientation of many of these public officials and organizations, it is not surprising that corporate executives, primarily from the 'Big Three,' were given a pretty significant say in how the region would respond.

The main labor representation in Detroit economic development decisions came through the United Auto Workers (UAW), one of the largest labor unions in North America. Though the UAW has seen a dramatic decline in membership since the automobile manufacturing sector's restructuring began in the 1970s, Detroit remains home to the UAW and has long held the reputation of being a union town. Initially, the UAW's involvement in regional issues generally put it on the defensive, as it deflected criticism about the high cost of doing business in Detroit. Over time, however, the UAW and other unions became involved in attempts to marry economic development efforts with workforce development efforts, ultimately becoming an important player in the decision-making process.

Within Detroit, reactions to the unfolding economic shift varied greatly. Local leaders, as well as the academic community, debated the nature and extent of this industrial shift (Bluestone and Harrison 1982; Lawrence 1982; Branson 1983). One interviewee, a state employee with the Department of Management and Budget during the 1970s and 1980s, described the uncertainty that unfolded as early reports about job losses trickled in.

> In the early 1980s, our field staff would come in with stories about GM and Ford, Chrysler closing a plant here or there and the potential impact. But again they were still doing so well; we didn't take it as a crisis. We knew there were looming issues but nobody thought the automobile industry would be in the shape that it is today, at that time. No one could believe it because they were so dominant with well over 50 percent of the market share in the 1980s. There was just not a feeling that that would lessen to the degree it has.

Another state official working within the Department of Commerce echoed these sentiments, noting that most people were unprepared for what unfolded in Detroit during the 1980s and beyond.

> I think few if any of us had any idea as to just how rapidly this would progress in the 80s, 90s, and into the twenty-first century. I don't think any of us saw that what was happening would result in the beginning of the twenty-first century being a transition from manufacturing to high-technology, knowledge-based, and information industries just as the previous century had seen the shift from agriculture to manufacturing. I think if you go back and compare . . . it is very similar to what happened at the beginning of the twentieth century, but I don't think we saw it at that point. I think we saw symptoms, but we weren't sure where it was going to lead us ultimately.

Having failed to reach any real consensus on the nature and extent of the industrial shift, local leaders devised a variety of strategies to combat associated job losses and relocations. As in many other manufacturing-dependent regions, local leaders in Detroit found that deciding which avenue to explore was not easy; it was a difficult task that many interviewees recalled grappling with at the time. One interviewee, a former employee of SEMCOG, described the ongoing debate within his organization.

> We had a lot of conversations centered around the question of whether we should throw all of our energies into saving the automobile-related jobs or put money behind other types of attraction strategies. In many ways, I think we all wanted to do both. But convincing ourselves that a combination of both was a good idea was a difficult task that I don't think was ever resolved.

The quandary that he describes is quite telling in that it summarizes the confusion about what could or should be done to ameliorate the problems that Detroit was experiencing. The belief remained steadfast that the manufacturing sector would ultimately rebound and employment in that industry would eventually resume former trajectories, and many Detroit-area efforts focused on retaining and expanding existing heavy manufacturing firms and largely ignored calls to diversify the industrial base. Recalling the figure-8 diagram from Chapter 2, it follows that the rigidity of this approach likely prolonged the Detroit region's conservation phase, a time in which stability trumps innovation. One Detroit-area academic with extensive knowledge of the ways in which localities responded to early warnings of the unfolding industrial shift found that:

> Michigan stakeholders didn't believe in industrial decline. They were a victim of their largeness and thought that they were immune to global fluctuations. Stakeholders were much more concerned with stretching their global tentacles than worrying about the threat of economic problems here in Detroit.

Though the respondents' reasoning sometimes differed, this sense of immunity and concern for increasing global market share was echoed by numerous interviewees. A former planner for the City of Detroit simply stated that, in response to economic changes, "non-action was the order of the day." This non-action may have referred only to the corporate-sector mentality of the time. While the 'Big Three' were hesitant to publicly acknowledge the industrial shift that seemed to be taking place, many of the other public stakeholders were not so timid in recognizing the impending challenges.

Within the city administration, the unfolding industrial shift was of great concern. One former official in the Department of Economic and Community Development noted that, in some ways, local leaders were galvanized by the threat of industrial extinction. Despite widespread recognition that the automobile industry was shrinking, the official described efforts – on the part of both public and union leaders – to willingly "reinforce an industry that was slowly getting smaller." This interviewee was not alone in expressing frustration at this conservative retention strategy. Numerous other interviewees mentioned their own misgivings about "committing too strongly to a recreation of history." Such fears were echoed in sentiments expressed by another interviewee – an activist working in Detroit during the latter half of the twentieth century – who reflected on the questions he was asking about the prevailing economic development strategy of the time.

> In a funny way, particularly in the late 1970s, there was very little emphasis on the workforce development issue. At first the issues were on tax abatement – in Michigan it was called Public Act 198 – and a lot of the questions around economic development issues revolved around what sorts of tax write-offs were given to companies as inducements to settle their large plants in the area.

Similar frustrations were described in relation to downtown redevelopment, which was another highly visible piece of the economic development strategy. Downtown Detroit in the 1980s, which was generally perceived as being an increasingly dangerous and unattractive place to recreate or live, was not often considered a desirable place for corporations to locate. One long-time real estate developer had this to say about the challenges that Detroit faced:

> In the early 80s, the downtown area was a scary place for many people. There was really no reason to be there. So, when 5:00 rolled around, people left and went back to their homes either in the suburbs or in other parts of town. No one really saw it as a place they wanted to be.

Given the pervasiveness of this negative perception, interviewees frequently alluded to the difficulty in trying to devise a strategy to increase the quality of life for the people of Detroit and the corporations headquartered there. One city planner described the process as follows:

> We knew we had to do something. People and companies were leaving Detroit in droves. We thought that the downtown needed shopping,

> sporting events, and high-end office space, but we didn't always agree on how it would get done. So, we did our best to do it. It took a long time but I think we got there.

Many of the efforts employed by stakeholders in Detroit did take a long time to execute, including the redevelopment of downtown Detroit through the construction of elements like the Renaissance Center – a group of seven mixed-use, interconnected skyscrapers on the Detroit River. Later investments included stadia, three casinos, and a revived Greektown. Though development does not always mean increased resilience, interviewees generally agreed that much of what was accomplished during this period did put Detroit in a better position than it would have been without this initial development and investment.

Despite its poor performance in traditional measures of the economy, Detroit remains one of America's largest regions and portions of it, mainly suburban areas, have fared quite well as measured through indicators like per capita income and educational attainment. For better or worse, the region also remains the American headquarters of automobile manufacturing in both a symbolic and a literal sense. The fact that it remains such a central player in the United States' economy and urban landscape suggests that, to some degree, parts of the region have exhibited adaptive resilience, albeit of the somewhat less traditional variety.

However, to say that Detroit overall has adapted well to the challenge of deindustrialization would not be appropriate. As we saw in Chapter 4, the region has not improved on most traditional measures of social or economic vitality, and employment losses continue to plague the region. If we then juxtapose the disappointing employment figures with the economic development strategies employed to improve these figures over time, we see that the economic development strategies have not successfully attracted or retained firms, nor increased employment in the longer term. The adaptive resilience perspective tells us that, in this sense, the Detroit region has not successfully adjusted to the challenges of deindustrialization because it has long hovered in the conservation and release quadrants and has not adapted well to changes in its economy over time.

Today, the public perception of Detroit is generally not a favorable one; newspaper headlines continue to announce further job and population losses and an unemployment rate of 9 percent, which ranks 44 of 49 among the country's largest metropolitan areas and is far higher than the national average of 7.3 percent (BLS 2013). Both a brief accounting of the economic history and accounts from local leaders corroborate the substantial challenges that the Detroit region has faced in recent decades. Despite such adversity, Detroit leaders remained optimistic about their ability to intervene and to improve on the local economy in a variety of ways. Interviewees described an array of responses at the state, regional, and local levels. Though the 'Betting on the Basics,' conservation-based approach seemed to work for a while – Detroit's productivity rebounded slightly during the 1990s – this automobile manufacturing-centric approach only temporarily masked fundamental weaknesses in the regional economy, many of which have reared their ugly heads again in recent years.

Milwaukee

Like the other regions that ultimately chose to 'Bet on the Basics,' the Milwaukee region was originally settled as a strategic transportation site due to its waterfront location. In addition to shipping, Milwaukee's early economic base included manufacturing, stockyards, and assorted heavy industry. Early on, the region was a distribution center for Midwestern agricultural produce, especially wheat grown in Wisconsin. Easy and plentiful access to Wisconsin's wheat, combined with large German and Polish populations, led to a large beer-brewing industry from the mid-1850s onward. Other industrial strengths included grain processing and storage, as well as tanneries and tool making.

Early strengths in brewing, processing, shipping, and manufacturing changed gradually over time; the brewing industry faded significantly by the 1970s and the region's manufacturing base continued to grow. In addition to general manufacturing production, the region's early strengths in tool making led to a local specialization in machine manufacturing and industrial controls. Early forays into these particular industries led to long-term specializations that would last for decades. A local economic development expert described how an early strength in tool making led to other, related sectoral strengths.

> Historically, we started with blacksmiths making tools and then the demand grew because agriculture grew to the west of here and they wanted more machines. So we started making machines to make machines, and then we needed mechanical controls for those machines, and then we needed electronic controls . . . That's how we came to account for much of the world market in industrial controls.

However, as was the case in so many other regions, success in one area of the economy did not always translate into success across the board. Tool making and then industrial controls has been one of the few easy successes seen in Milwaukee. The region experienced largely unfettered growth up until the 1970s. Thereafter, leaders watched as manufacturing jobs disappeared in droves. During the 1980s, the region suffered considerably as firms downsized or closed altogether. A former council member described these turbulent times.

> There certainly was concern. The recessions hurt and then the migrations outward certainly had an impact. People were aware of these. There were just a number of companies that closed their doors, many of them larger employers in the region. In the early 1980s, Babcock and Wilcox made

> pipes for nuclear reactors in West Allis. Then they closed and 1,200 jobs [were lost]. The biggest single employer was Allis-Chalmers. They made turbines and tractors, farm equipment, a host of products and they were always second, third, or fourth in where they stood in any given market. Their heyday in West Allis had 17,500 workers there. They shuttered in 1985. Even in brewing, Schlitz Brewing, the beer that made Milwaukee famous, disappeared in 1986 or 1987 and that was another 4,000 jobs.

In reaction to these significant and highly visible losses, leaders embarked on an aggressive agenda to retain manufacturing and bolster the economy against future challenges. During the 1970s and 1980s, the region fought to remain in the conservation phase by 'Betting on the Basics.' This approach was likely prioritized because attraction strategies – the hallmark of approaches like 'Bidding Down,' 'Bowing Out,' and 'Sharing the Wealth' – were not really feasible in Wisconsin. A former suburban mayor described why this was the case.

> The difficulty is that Wisconsin doesn't play in the incentives game. It has very few tools. Part of the state constitution says everyone will be taxed the same. So, you can't forgive taxes coming in the way many states do. So, we have TIFs [Tax Increment Financing], a few other things [that] can be done – some training incentives and the like . . . In Wisconsin, we stand no chance on the attraction . . . I cannot name a company, nor can anyone else, that has moved to southeastern Wisconsin in the last 25 or 30 years.

Having so few tools in hand to help attract companies, Milwaukee leaders instead chose to focus on the areas of the economy in which they perceived they had an advantage. Interviewees suggested that the strong commitment to manufacturing, or at least to high-tech varieties of manufacturing, stemmed from the fact that there was plentiful vacant industrial land within the city of Milwaukee and a highly skilled workforce across the region as a whole. While the abundant land would come about later through policy changes, the presence of a skilled workforce was likely the result of both local culture and political intervention. As the former suburban mayor noted, the workforce was seen as a real asset during the struggles of the 1970s and 1980s.

> We have had a very skilled workforce. We certainly have a large unskilled workforce, but the skilled workforce had a terrific work ethic. I've talked with lots of CEOs and Human Relations folks who mention the work ethic of Milwaukee workers . . . So this was a selling point. And the skill levels were high. We've got a lot of people who know how to make things.

Though these experienced workers could not do much to attract firms, they were a large part of the reason that firms either stayed or grew their businesses in the Milwaukee region. Maintaining this skilled workforce was part of the strategy that local leaders employed in their 'Betting on the Basics' response. As one local educator noted,

> Wisconsin has a very strong technical college system. I think we've got 14 technical colleges spread around the state. The largest one is in Milwaukee; it's called Milwaukee Technical College.

Workforce development efforts like the technical colleges have historically been a significant part of Milwaukee's history (Fung and Zdrazil 2004). In the wake of economic restructuring in the 1970s and 1980s, these efforts were also an important component in the economic development response seen in Milwaukee. Nevertheless, leaders were not so naïve as to think that a skilled workforce would be the only thing needed to grow or retain firms. Numerous other efforts were also made to market the Milwaukee region as a good place for heavy industry to do business.

Rast (2009) argues that annexation was the first of many steps that the region took towards creating a more hospitable environment for businesses. An aggressive annexation program, which started in the 1940s and 1950s, really took shape in 1960 with the election of Democrat Henry Maier as mayor of Milwaukee. Maier's main economic development initiative was to use the annexed land for industrial land banking as a way to ensure that there would always be a large supply of vacant industrial land ready for firms looking to expand specifically within the city (Ibid.). Because a penchant for sprawling, single-story plants materialized during the 1970s and 1980s, the land banking approach to industrial development ended up being a pretty good bet for the city of Milwaukee, and thus for the region as a whole.

Given that land banking was a relatively new phenomenon at that point in time and given that the upfront expenses of this approach were so high, one can appreciate just how risky this type of initiative may have felt back in the 1960s and 1970s. Nevertheless, interviewees frequently mentioned this approach as being one of the most important economic development tools used in the Milwaukee region. As one current city official noted,

> It took a long time to be successful. The basic notion I think has some merit because it did allow the city to be competitive. It had parcels. It developed them in ways, put in the infrastructure. So when manufacturers make that last-minute decision that they have to expand, [they] could buy and build in a short period of time. But since there was so little activity in the 1980s, we were getting smaller rather than larger, this land sat for a period of time, quite a while. In the 1990s, business picked up and we had some demand. It grew. The first part of the 1990s is probably some of the best growth we saw in a while.

In time, land banking for the purposes of industrial and economic development occurred in both the city and the suburbs. In both cases, it generally occurred on land that had been purchased, cleared, and subsequently 'banked' by the public sector. As one public sector leader noted, this type of investment was not an easy one.

> Had we known what we were getting ourselves into – because there were environmental issues and the potential that we might not be able to sell the property to recoup the cost of the investment – would we still do it today? At the time, we saw little other options. We knew that the private sector was not going to invest their money into these properties. If there were going to be any expansions, if firms were going to expand, they were going out west, up north into the greenfield areas, rather than into our brownfields . . . So, we thought that in order to be able to retain businesses, we had to do a number of things like banking the land, and spending money on roads, water, and sewers.

Though the land banking industrial development approach does not fit cleanly within the parameters of the 'Betting on the Basics' approach that Markusen and Carlson (1988) describe, it undoubtedly reflects a desire on the part of Milwaukee leaders to bolster employment in the troubled urban core and make at least this part of the region a more attractive place for large manufacturers to do business. Because of the risk involved – both financially and politically – the Milwaukee region represents one of the few cases where the leadership took a risk in 'Betting on the Basics.'

The Milwaukee region's retention-based strategy was perhaps more holistic in approach than that of other 'Basic Betters.' The region's focus on workforce development, annexation, and land banking represents a broad, multifaceted attempt to hold on to the manufacturing base and to retain or expand firms already in the region. The land banking approach was a fairly new and risky approach when Milwaukee implemented it during the 1970s. This risk, however, did not immediately pay off for the region, as evidenced by its prolonged and painful response period. Over time, however, Milwaukee revealed itself as somewhat of an outlier in that it was the only region to 'Bet on the Basics' and also experience multiple 'good outcomes,' including population and employment growth during the response period. Despite these small wins, the region continues to face substantial difficulty in the wake of deindustrialization and still remains a manufacturing-intensive economy.

Cleveland

Cleveland's early rise to prominence as a center of industry revolved around its strategic location at the nexus of the Cuyahoga River and Lake Erie. Beyond transportation, early strengths were in steel, with a specific focus on primary metals, fabricated metals, non-electrical machinery, electrical machinery, and transportation equipment. Like so many other manufacturing-intensive regions, the Cleveland economy underwent significant restructuring in the latter half of the twentieth century. Cleveland began confronting significant challenges in the 1950s, many of which would continue through the 1980s and beyond. Between 1967 and 1977, one in seven manufacturing jobs was lost (Rand Corporation 1982, 7). Continuing challenges resulted in a loss of nearly 18,000 manufacturing jobs between 1976 and 1984 alone (Krumholz and Forester 1990, 16). The biggest losses were seen in primary metals, electrical and nonelectrical machinery, and transportation equipment (Rand Corporation 1982). Increases in non-manufacturing employment helped to counter these losses but many of these new jobs were in lower-paying positions. Overall, non-manufacturing employment growth contributed to a slight increase in total employment but growth occurred at a much slower rate than the national average.

The Cleveland region also confronted major demographic changes during this time. Up until the 1970s, population had continually grown at a moderate pace. Intra-region population shifts accounted for some population losses in the inner core but growth in the suburbs generally was enough to offset any losses seen in the inner city. Total population losses began during the 1970s, when the Cleveland metropolitan area lost about 150,000 people, or 6.5 percent of its total population. Outmigration continued through the 1980s, when another 68,000 people left the region. The region's population would stabilize in the 1990s but has not recovered to its peak level of 1970.

Early warnings of economic restructuring combined with ongoing population outmigration in the 1970s and 1980s caused growing concern for Cleveland's leaders. In 1982, regional leaders were so concerned with these emerging problems that the Cleveland Foundation commissioned an assessment of economic and population trends by the Rand Corporation, entitled "The Cleveland Metropolitan Economy: An Initial Assessment." The report's purpose was to gain "a better understanding of how the metropolitan Cleveland economy works, what its special role has been in the U.S. economy, and how it has been responding to a changing economic environment" (Rand Corporation 1982, iii). In the Executive Summary of this assessment, the authors optimistically describe a changing Cleveland economy.

> Cleveland's slow rate of total employment growth does not necessarily suggest a stagnant regional economy. The more detailed figures indicate only that the Cleveland metropolitan economy is a mature but still quite dynamic economic system.
>
> (9)

The authors specifically point to the slowing of steel manufacturing as evidence of a maturing economy for the region as a whole, adding that many of the more recent challenges also stemmed from the region's close ties to the automobile industry. Much of the early economic growth in Cleveland was linked to the automobile industry because the region's steel mills sold most of their output to automobile production firms. Still, the Rand report showed that Cleveland was less sensitive to fluctuations in the automobile industry than were other metropolitan regions like Pittsburgh and Indianapolis (Rand Corporation 1982). Though the authors admit that Cleveland's economy in the 1970s was not all that diverse, "Cleveland production serving other markets cushioned the shocks of swings in demand from the automobile sector" (Ibid., 14).

To the extent that this diversity may have lessened the blows of cyclical fluctuations in the economy, such cushioning may have also masked the emerging challenges that Cleveland would soon confront as a result of widespread economic restructuring. Unlike other regions where manufacturing losses were sudden and sharp, Cleveland's early losses were less severe. As such, leaders had less incentive to consider alternative development scenarios. One economic development official with the City of Cleveland recalled an over-arching commitment to a 'Betting on the Basics'-type economic development response.

> I think at that time we were still hoping to hold on to the heavy industrial pattern of the past: steel, metal bending (particularly in automobiles), tool and die work, chemicals, paints, varnishes . . . Those were the older industries that had been very productive in the past, and the city was still trying to hold its place with those industries.

Interviewees frequently described how early response efforts did in fact align with a 'Betting on the Basics' approach, focusing largely on retaining manufacturing firms in the region. However, as one former council member described, losses seen in the steel industry indicated that this approach was not working.

> By the late 1970s, it was apparent that we were losing industries. I think in the early 1970s we had four steel manufacturing facilities: US Steel, Jones and Laughlin, New Republic's world headquarters, and one other. Early in the 1970s, two of them closed down or merged, so we began to lose jobs in steel. We were very conscious of the local loss of population, and we were increasingly very conscious of the fact that the existing population was very poor. We weren't helping anyone by trying to hold on to these dying facilities.

It was around this time that support grew for a more progressive approach to economic development. Calls for an equity-driven approach came largely from the City of Cleveland Planning Commission. The Commission during this time advocated "not for the business community but for 'those people in Cleveland who had few if any choices,' for poor and working-class city residents" (Krumholz and Forester 1990, xix). During the 1970s and early 1980s, the Commission made it its goal to provide employment opportunities for residents so that they could feed their children, to provide transportation for residents to get to their jobs, and to ensure that affordable housing was available to rent or buy. The Commission's efforts were by no means an official representation of the region's approach *as a whole*, but its highly visible and often successful initiatives made it a major player at the decision-making table and ensured that the 'Sharing the Wealth' approach was at least heard. Much of its efforts, however, did not manifest in terms of economic development within the Cleveland region.

Suburban areas undoubtedly saw things from a different perspective. As one suburban county planner noted, outer portions of the region were experiencing changes of a different sort.

> We, in the suburbs, were doing pretty well. We were the recipients of most of the outmigration and disinvestment that was taking place in the city. Until very recently, the suburbs . . . were not suffering from many of the problems that the city was suffering from. In general, the income in suburban jurisdictions was substantially higher than in the city.

Though this interviewee does not mention it, racial disparity within the region was also on the rise. As outmigration was occurring, so too was a region-wide racial sorting of the population. While most of the white population moved outward to the more prosperous suburbs, minorities remained in the central city and the region gradually became one of the most segregated in the country.

Though they were far removed from the everyday challenges of the inner city, suburban constituents with jobs in the central city still cared that the region as a whole remained strong and stable. Similar to the response seen in Milwaukee, one of the main regional development efforts to come out of this period was the development of a land bank, which would allow the city to take title of and subsequently to land-bank tax-delinquent and abandoned properties. Creation of the land bank required changing local, county, and state laws. Interviewees noted that such changes would not have been possible without the formation of a regional effort. A planner from Cuyahoga County said that,

> Coalitions were very important for setting up a land bank. We had to study the problem of tax abandonment and change the state law on the ownership of real estate, and you don't do that without a coalition. We set up a coalition both across the state and across the region to accomplish that. None of this would have been done without region-wide support.

In the end, the Cleveland region exhibited an interesting and multi-faceted response to deindustrialization. After experiencing low levels of manufacturing job losses, the region slowly began to respond to the impending restructuring. Region-wide, early efforts aligned most closely with the 'Betting on the Basics' approach, marked by a strong commitment to retaining existing heavy industry and a prolonged period in what could be described as the conservation phase. Later efforts, primarily in the city, coalesced around the issue of equity and the creation of an economy and a community that was more accessible to all of Cleveland's residents.

Buffalo

In Buffalo, 'Betting on the Basics' felt a little less like a choice and more like an inevitable fate. Early sectoral strengths in grain storage, steel production, railroad and shipping commerce, automobile production, aerospace design, and construction brought the Buffalo region great prosperity in the early 1900s. All that changed during the latter half of the twentieth century, as the region began to confront a series of formidable challenges.

Among the more devastating changes was the opening of the St. Lawrence Seaway in 1959, which made water-based travel through Buffalo considerably less relevant. While Buffalo grappled with these changes in transportation routes, it also confronted its own problems related to the national fundamental economic restructuring trend. The region, which had long been dependent on heavy manufacturers and related industries, had to deal with a maturing steel industry on top of this broader economic slowdown. In the 1970s, Buffalo steel manufacturers were increasingly strained by foreign competition, aging technology, and excess capacity. Such challenges contributed to a massive and painful restructuring across the Buffalo region's economy. One former Erie County official said of his outlook at that time,

> Everybody needs steel . . . and for a company to start saying we are not going to make as much steel as we used to, we are going to cut down not only Buffalo, but other plants . . . it was pretty traumatic. Not only were the numbers bad in terms of layoffs and the ancillary ripple effects, it was especially traumatic because [we felt] something was happening and it was a hard thing to take.

The severity of this restructuring became abundantly clear in 1977 when Bethlehem Steel, a major employer in the Buffalo region, took a $740 million dollar write-off and shut down most of its local operations. Within three years, Bethlehem Steel closed its foundry and twelve-inch bar mill operations. Republic Steel also cut about 2,500 jobs. Overall, the 1970s and 1980s were a time of substantial job losses in steel and manufacturing in general. Most of the significant losses occurred between 1979 and 1986, when 45,000 manufacturing jobs – one-third of the manufacturing jobs in the region – disappeared. Unsurprisingly, unemployment for the region as a whole (9.6 percent) ran significantly higher than the national average (7.6 percent) during this period (Dillaway 2006).

Compounding the troubles of significant regional job losses in the manufacturing sector and high unemployment overall were the related problems of population outmigration, a decaying downtown, inadequate infrastructure, pronounced white flight to the suburbs, emerging racial tensions, and highly segregated schools (Ibid.). From 1970 to 1980, Buffalo lost almost 95,000 people or 5 percent of the total population (US Census of Population and Housing 1970, 1980). Job losses similarly made local leaders increasingly concerned about the future of steel in Buffalo and the viability of the Buffalo regional economy as a whole. As Kraushaar and Perry (1990) put it, "the Buffalo economy was a perfect example of a region dedicated to and dependent on a mature industrial base" (50). Despite such dependence, Buffalo leaders from the private and public sectors did attempt to address these problems in a variety of ways.

Buffalo is an interesting case because, unlike many of the other regions in this study, its early leadership came largely from the public sector. As Dillaway notes, power often resided with the political leadership "because elite organizations did not provide proactive leadership in Buffalo's political and economic debates" (2006, 133). Though all of that would change in the late 1980s, much of the early response to deindustrialization was indeed crafted by local politicians. Among the most influential strategies employed was the commissioning of a study, "Buffalo Area Economic Readjustment Strategy," by Arthur D. Little Consultants in 1978. The report card-like study was commissioned by the Erie County Industrial Development Authority (ECIDA) and supported by Mayor Griffin, who wanted to provide leaders with a framework for moving forward. A former economic development official had this to say about the study's findings:

> It found over-concentration in steel and found some real problems in terms of labor-management relations. We were a union town, lots of negative implications . . . and a lot of strike problems that were giving the area a bad reputation. We had a very fragmented economic development scene with multiple agencies sometimes working at cross-purposes or too many people trying to do the same thing without any coordination. So the report card was pretty stark in terms of [Buffalo] being on a bad road and not terribly well-equipped to deal with it . . . A plan for attempting to deal with it came out of [this report], which really became the blueprint for economic development over the next 15 years or so.

One of the main findings from the study was the recommendation that local leaders essentially write off the ailing steel industry and focus instead on retaining other industrial firms that were still active in the regional economy. The end goal of the study was to make the region self-sufficient by guiding it through long-term changes in its basic economic structure. The study provided recommendations for how the ECIDA could reach out and assist the firms that were experiencing difficulties, as well as firms that were considering expansion. Because only Erie County, and not Niagara County, was part of ECIDA's jurisdiction, responses crafted in regards to the Arthur

D. Little study primarily pertained to Erie County and the city of Buffalo. A former head of the ECIDA described this assistance process.

> We had a staff of four and their job was to knock on doors . . . The goal was to call on every single company every two years and explain to them what we could offer to try to get things going. When you called on a company, you uncovered one of two things. One is that you uncover retention problems with companies at risk, either ready to take flight or disinvest. At least you can get them on your watch list and start dealing with them. The second thing is that you find the ones that, given the right incentives or given the right means of correcting some of the diseconomies they were facing in the Buffalo area, might actually put a shovel in the ground and expand.

This focus on retention strategies was one of the many ways in which the Arthur D. Little study influenced local decisions during the late 1970s and early 1980s. In a sense, the authors of the study recommended that the region try to adapt by 'turning the corner' from the rigidity of the conservation phase into the creative destruction of release. However, making this transition was not easy for regional leaders and they were largely unsuccessful in the end.

Another important development that stemmed from the study's recommendations was the creation of the Buffalo-Erie County Labor Management Council. Again, this effort was primarily focused on Buffalo and Erie County, not Niagara Falls or Niagara County. The group was formed largely in response to the tremendous ongoing problems between labor and management in the Buffalo region. As a former member of the council describes:

> The council was created to attempt to deal with the union situation, the large number of strikes, the labor–management animosity that was present in town, the reputation that the Buffalo area had for being a heavy union town. If you were going to come and do business there you better be prepared to take a strike every once in a while and deal with it. The council's charge was to get in the middle of sensitive labor–management issues as neither management nor labor, but as an independent entity affiliated loosely with the ECIDA; someone who could just be an independent broker and arbiter. It was also an attempt to get more settlements without strikes and to attempt to change the reputation of the area.

Despite such lofty goals, the group was only marginally successful at mediating a number of strikes and settling several major grievances (Dillaway 2006, 117). Interviewees, however, frequently made note of the lingering challenges associated with a heavily unionized economy.

Beyond the ECIDA, numerous other public sector players also weighed in with their own economic development responses. One of the most visible responses came from City Hall, when Mayor Griffin formed the Buffalo-Erie County Regional Development Corporation in 1978. This group, largely consisting of community development professionals, was designed to be a lending corporation that would give the public sector the ability to support innovative business initiatives in Buffalo. More importantly, the formation of this corporation was an important step towards creating a public-private partnership and bringing business leaders into the fold. One interviewee, a former state economic development official, described the need for private sector involvement.

> We pulled together the steel companies . . . we did a lot of that stuff. But really we couldn't get a lot going. It was an investment issue. The public sector was really willing to do a lot but we needed the private sector.

Ongoing efforts amongst the business community ended up being an important part of the Buffalo story, especially in light of a significant shift that occurred amongst the regional leadership in the late 1970s. The shift occurred in part because of an infusion of new leaders who came from outside of the region and were highly entrepreneurial (Perry 1990). Amongst the newcomers were Ross Kensie, brought in to head Goldome Bank; Stanford Lipsey, publisher of the *Buffalo Evening News*; and Robert Wilmers, head of M and T Bank. These three joined with other members of the business elite to form the Buffalo 18, a powerful group of executives who worked together to assume control of the Greater Buffalo Development Foundation, a smallish group of business leaders; the Chamber of Commerce; and various other local groups. Members included heads of all the major regional banks, manufacturers, and service sector firms. In total, the Buffalo 18 included 17 CEOs and the president of the region's largest university (Ibid.). A former Director of the Western New York Economic Development Corporation (WNYEDC) said that,

> With the Gang of 18, you knew you were dealing with a powerful group. When they made up their mind on something, it usually happened. You could only be in this group if you could be counted on to make things happen.

Ultimately, the group did make things happen, primarily by infiltrating the boards of various local organizations and funding the recruitment of key personnel from outside the region. Such maneuvers were useful in the sense that they helped formulate the critical mass needed to devise a plan to move the region forward. Implementation of this plan, however, was not entirely successful.

Collaborating with this group were certain state government officials and select elected officials. The WNYEDC was an important part of the recovery strategy, providing project assistance, industrial modernization, and targeting clusters that had the potential to be globally competitive (Kossy 1996). At this point in time, cluster analysis focused primarily on a burgeoning medical corridor and leveraging some local assets for tourism development. For the most part, WNYEDC provided long-term strategic planning for the regional economy as a whole and helped guide the development process for certain larger projects. These types of larger projects, including waterfront development and a mass transit line, were generally considered embarrassing failures and did little to help the region's recovery process. Even with support from the nation's first Urban Development Action Grant and millions of dollars in Community Development Block Grants, the results did little to change or disrupt the region's trajectory.

In the end, most of these valiant efforts did little to help the Buffalo region gain traction. Alternative approaches seemed implausible as efforts to attract outside firms proved unsuccessful. Retention strategies were slightly more effective but generally not productive enough to stave off decline. Ultimately, the challenges facing Buffalo were larger than anyone had previously thought. A former city official in the city's economic development department summarized it best when he said:

> The manufacturing and durable industries were restructuring and the plants in Buffalo were old and inefficient. The workforce was inefficient. Buffalo was going through a long period of structural economic decline. It was cold. It wasn't an attractive location. That was kind of the longer-term challenge.

Indeed, these longer-term challenges continue today. Buffalo remains a region that has struggled greatly to adapt to the challenges of the late twentieth and early twenty-first centuries. Its retention-based strategy – 'Betting on the Basics' – was not enough to counter the region's massive industrial restructuring, move the region beyond the conservation and release phases, or improve the negative image of Buffalo as a whole.

Conclusions

Though their experiences varied substantially and all had different assets and opportunities at the start, all four case study regions chose to place their bets primarily on manufacturing by 'Betting on the Basics.' In each region, the gamble had a slightly different outcome; however, in the end, none would be considered the epitome of adaptive resilience. From these case studies emerge a series of observations about similarities across these regions and ruminations on the effectiveness of 'Betting on the Basics' in response to deindustrialization. Observations and lessons follow below.

Together with supporting quantitative data, the interview data aided in the identification of three common characteristics across these four regions.

First, findings suggest that all of these regions were heavily dependent on manufacturing, both psychologically and economically. Although we already know from Chapter 4 that these four regions were most dependent on manufacturing as a percent of total employment, the numbers say little, if anything, about the nature of that dependence. Interviewees from these four regions frequently described a situation in which regional leaders (and their constituents) had difficulty envisioning an economy that did not rely on manufacturing as their region's primary economic base. In other words, leaders found it difficult to either personally envision a future that moved away from such dependence or convince their constituents, customers, or employees of such an alternative future. Though that may have also been the case in *some* of the other regions in this study, it is true for *all four* of the regions that ultimately subscribed to the 'Betting on the Basics' ideology.

Second, all of these regions, with the exception of Milwaukee, were heavily dependent on manufacturing jobs of a certain type: steel production and bending. For many interviewees, being so entwined in the fate of one particular sector of manufacturing was significant; it often created a sense of community and brought with it the understanding that most families' wellbeing would rise and fall with the success of the steel industry. Hourly wages were much higher for steel production than other manufacturing jobs: 14.04 versus 8.33 dollars per hour in 1978, respectively (Crandall 1981, 90). Thus, many of these regions faced great difficulty when the global steel market collapsed during the mid- to late 1970s in the wake of the 1973 oil crisis and the market became increasingly saturated. As a result of this collapse, many steel mills in the United States Rust Belt were shuttered and many jobs were lost. Thus, for many Rust Belt regions, the decline of steel production and the loss of so many of these high-paying jobs would become the defining feature of their regional economy in the 1970s and 1980s. It seems fitting, then, that the majority of the regions that experienced such extreme losses might react similarly, in this case by 'Betting on the Basics.'

Third, all of these regions are located on the shores of one of the Great Lakes and none is their state's capital. It is beyond the scope of this study to determine whether there is a relationship between shorelines and economic growth. However, it seems plausible that those regions that share a border with one of the Great Lakes might experience higher levels of lake-effect snowfall and lower levels of desirability or longer and deeper histories of heavy industry as a result. Without specifying causation, it is worth noting that *all* of the regions that elected to 'Bet on the Basics' are located on one of these lakes. *All* of these regions are also non-capital cities, meaning that their labor markets might be less diverse and less stable than those of their capital counterparts, where state government employment and capital act as a buffer against economic challenges (Markusen 1996). Determining causation in this regard is again beyond the scope of this study. Nevertheless, establishing this link between these traits and the propensity to 'Bet on the Basics' may prove useful in future research.

Lessons learned

Turning now towards lessons we might draw from these case studies, two main points emerge. The first is that 'Betting on the Basics,' despite Markusen and Carlson's prediction, generally did not bode well for the regions that subscribed to it. Detroit, Milwaukee, Cleveland, and Buffalo and all suffered greatly as deindustrialization unfolded and in the years that followed. Though some of these regions fared better than others and certain manufacturing corporations successfully weathered the storm, this approach as a whole did not benefit regions in the way that it was predicted to. Perhaps in anticipation of this potential disappointing outcome, Markusen and Carlson (1988) offered a warning about the difficulty in successfully executing this retention-based approach: "Any retention strategy which works will have to tackle the reticence of many Midwestern manufacturers to revamp their labor relations systems, to develop strategic planning, to engage in technological experimentation, and to market aggressively" (33). In Markusen and Carlson's opinion, then, it is perhaps not the fault of the regions for choosing to 'Bet on the Basics' so much as it is the fault of the corporations for failing to adjust to new economic realities. Nevertheless, the outcomes were not generally good for these regions or the firms that called them home.

Second, analysis of these interviews and related data suggest that the 'Betting on the Basics' approach was not often associated with adaptive resilience or with 'good outcomes.' As Pendall et al. (2010) remind us, a reed is generally most resilient, or least breakable, when it bends. Likewise, adaptive resilience theory tells us that a region should experience the greatest levels of resilience when it, as a system, exhibits flexibility in a time of great flux. Flexible would not be the most appropriate way to describe the process of change in Detroit, Milwaukee, Cleveland, or Buffalo. To be certain, each of these regions did attempt to bend in its own way. Detroit activists tried to change the direction of economic development funding and prioritize a more equitable approach to development. In Buffalo, we saw the commissioning of the Arthur D. Little study and the formation of the Buffalo-Erie County Labor Management Council. In Cleveland, leaders working in the City of Cleveland Planning Commission fought diligently for transportation and employment opportunities to support the disenfranchised. And in Milwaukee, leaders came up with a creative solution to encourage development in the urban core. In the end, however, all four of these regions are known less for their progressive ideals or their creative solutions than they are for their failure to adjust to the new realities of the post-industrial economy. If flexibility is indeed a positive attribute that is necessary for adaptive resilience and 'good outcomes,' we can be fairly certain that these four regions did little in the way of encouraging it. By 'Betting on the Basics,' these regions either ignored calls to diversify their economic base or lacked the tools and assets necessary to heed the warning. For most of these regions, 'Betting on the Basics' (either by default or by choice) created an inflexible reed that ultimately made adaptation and 'good outcomes' a lot more difficult to achieve in the years to come.

References

Bachelor, Lynn W. 1998. "Stadiums as Solution Sets: Baseball, Football and the Revival of Downtown Detroit." *Policy Studies Review* 15(1): 89–101.

BLS. 2013. "Local Area Unemployment." Accessed March 12, 2014. http://www.bls.gov/web/metro/laulrgma.htm.

Bluestone, Barry, and Bennett Harrison. 1982. *The Deindustrialization of America*. New York: Basic Books.

Branson, William. 1983. "Myth of De-industrialization." *Regulation* 7(5): 24–29.

Crandall, Robert W. 1981. *The U.S. Steel Industry in Recurrent Crisis*. Washington, DC: Brookings Institution Press.

DiGaetano, Joe, and Paul Lawless. 1999. "Urban Governance and Industrial Decline: Governing Structures and Policy Agendas in Birmingham and Sheffield, England, and Detroit, Michigan, 1980–1997." *Urban Affairs Review* 34(4): 546–577.

Dillaway, Diana. 2006. *Power Failure: Politics, Patronage, and the Economic Future of Buffalo, New York*. Amherst, NY: Prometheus.

Farley, Reynolds, Sheldon Danziger, and Harry L. Holzer. 2000. *Detroit Divided*. New York: Russell Sage.

Fung, Archon, and Scott Zdrazil. 2004. "Ecologies of Workforce Development in Milwaukee." In *Workforce Development Politics: Civic Capacity and Performance*, edited by Robert P. Giloth, 75–101. Philadelphia, PA: Temple University Press.

Ingrassia, Paul, and Joseph B. White. 1995. *Comeback: The Fall and Rise of the American Automobile Industry*. New York: Simon and Schuster.

Jo, Hyung Je. 2002. "Regional Restructuring and Urban Regimes: A Comparison of the Pittsburgh and Detroit Metropolitan Areas." Office for the Study of Automotive Transportation University of Michigan Transportation Research Institute, UMTRI 2002–20.

Kossy, Judith. 1996. "Economic Restructuring and the Restructuring of Economic Development Practice: A New York Perspective, 1985–1995." *Economic Development Quarterly* 10(4): 300–314.

Kraushaar, Robert, and David Perry. 1990. "Buffalo, New York: Region of No Illusions." In *Economic Restructuring of the American Midwest: Proceedings of the Midwest Economic Restructuring Conference of the Federal Reserve Bank of Cleveland*, edited by Richard D. Bingham and Randall W. Eberts, 47–74. New York: Springer-Verlag.

Krumholz, Norman and John Forester. 1990. *Making Equity Planning Work*. Philadelphia, PA: Temple University Press.

Lawrence, Robert Z. 1982. "Deindustrialization and U.S. International Competitiveness: Domestic and International Forces in U.S. Industrial Performance, 1970–1980." Washington, DC: The Brookings Institution.

Markusen, Ann. 1996. "Sticky Places in Slippery Space: A Typology of Industrial Districts." *Economic Geography* 72(3): 293–313.

Markusen, Ann, and Virginia Carlson. 1988. "Bowing Out, Bidding Down, and Betting on the Basics: Midwestern Responses to Deindustrialization in the 1980s." *Center for Urban Affairs and Policy Research*, Working Paper, Northeastern University, Boston, MA.

Pendall, Rolf, Kathryn Foster, and Margaret Cowell. 2010. "Resilience and Regions: Building Understanding of the Metaphor." *Cambridge Journal of Regions, Economy and Society* 3(1): 71–84.

Perry, David. 1990. "Recasting Urban Leadership in Buffalo." In *Leadership and Urban Regeneration: Cities in North American and Europe,* edited by Dennis Judd and Michael Parkinson, 258–276. London, UK: Sage.

Rand Corporation. 1982. "The Cleveland Metropolitan Economy: An Initial Assessment." Aaron Gurwitz and G. Thomas Kingsley, eds.

Rast, Joel. 2009. "Critical Junctures, Long-Term Processes: Urban Redevelopment in Chicago and Milwaukee, 1945–1980." *Social Science History* 33(4): 393–426.

Rich, Wilbur C. 1989. *Coleman Young and Detroit Politics: From Social Activist to Power Broker*. Detroit, MI: Wayne State University Press.

U.S. Census. 1970. Census of Population and Housing. Series P2 (PC(P2)-32). Accessed April 6, 2010. http://www2.census.gov/prod2/decennial/documents/026655922.pdf.

U.S. Census. 1980. Census of Population and Housing. Series 2 (PHC80–2–106). Accessed April 6, 2010. http://www2.census.gov/prod2/decennial/documents/1980/tracts-cities/CensusTracts1980-BuffaloNY.pdf.

6 'Bowing Out'

Cincinnati, Pittsburgh, Indianapolis, and Columbus

In the face of an unfolding challenge like deindustrialization, many regions chose to stick with what they knew either because it felt safe, seemed easiest, or was thought to be the only option available. In Detroit, Milwaukee, Cleveland, and Buffalo, leaders did just that – they 'Bet on the Basics' and focused most of their efforts on maintaining manufacturing. For other regions – namely, Cincinnati, Pittsburgh, Indianapolis, and Columbus – that had both the will and the means to take a different approach, regional leaders took steps to consciously move beyond what was easiest and familiar, in hopes of reaching a better outcome. For the most part, the 'Bowing Out' approach meant looking for alternatives, something different from the manufacturers of yore. For many of these regions, investing in alternative approaches did pay off and the regional response to deindustrialization ensured favorable outcomes. In others, regional outcomes were not as positive. In this chapter I explain how leaders in Cincinnati, Pittsburgh, Indianapolis, and Columbus arrived at the decision to explore alternatives, and discuss the extent to which doing so helped or hindered their region's future prospects. I begin with Cincinnati, a region whose response was to somewhat passively focus on diversification, which ultimately helped it to 'turn the corner.'

Cincinnati

Cincinnati's regional economy saw significant growth in the production of pork, beer, soap, machine tools, and carriages during the early twentieth century (Stradling 2003). Though the breweries and carriage production would largely taper off, firms specializing in meatpacking, soap-making, and machine tool production would continue to fuel the regional economy through much of the twentieth century. Cincinnati, which at one point was nicknamed Porkopolis, was the central processing point for pig farmers in Ohio, Indiana, and beyond. Pigs would be brought into the region to be processed and packaged for shipment to other parts of the country. Incidentally, soap-making began as a way to utilize the lard by-product from pork processing. One of Cincinnati's most important corporations – Procter and Gamble – initially began as a soap manufacturing firm in 1837. As one former city council member said, it remains one of the region's most powerful and productive firms today.

> P and G is the key company. The things P and G wants, it gets . . . It's a very thoughtful company and, fortunately, an enlightened company with great leadership. The community benefits from that.

Because of its rather diverse assortment of industrial strengths, Cincinnati was not as dependent on heavy industry as many other Midwestern regions. One former business leader in the region described how this diversity benefited the region.

> We never really felt wholly dependent on one corporation or one sector. Looking back, I don't think we realized how lucky we were to not be the auto town or the steel town. We definitely struggled in our own way but it probably wasn't as bad as it could have been.

So, as other regions grappled with severe losses in heavy industry, Cincinnati buried its head and plodded forward. An industrial base rooted in consumer goods and transportation helped the region to weather the stormy 1980s recessions. The region did, however, contend with many of the same land use problems as its peers. During the mid-twentieth century, many of Cincinnati's largest companies moved outward from the urban core in search of larger plots of land for their single-story plants. Even though the region felt fewer effects as a result of economic restructuring during the late 1970s and early 1980s, it still felt the effects of the national recessions and grappled with an outward dispersion of people and capital (Spring 1984). As one former county commissioner noted, these centrifugal forces created an acrimonious political environment.

> The central county was decreasing while the outlying counties were growing bigger. The city was in competition with the rest of the county. The county commissioners were seen as anti-city and pro part of the county. That was a real problem because we couldn't get a whole lot done and we didn't always cooperate.

In spite of these difficulties, leaders in the central city did make an effort to respond to unfolding challenges, namely a decaying downtown and a hollowing-out of the inner core. A former mayor during the early 1980s described one such effort.

> About that time, we commissioned a study called Cincinnati 2000. It was a ULI [Urban Land Institute] study that we commissioned to recommend to us what we should do about our core area . . . It urged us to concentrate on downtown living. We sort of ran afoul of the corporate chamber attitude, which was that we ought to continue to be a shopping destination and that we ought to be building more office buildings and maybe a few people would live downtown. I think the ULI had it correct.

During the 1980s, as leaders grappled with abandonment in the downtown area, tensions grew between those who supported downtown living, those who desired downtown shopping, and those who wanted to ignore the downtown and focus on booming suburban areas instead. The Cincinnati 2000 plan, which urged support for increased residential opportunities downtown, never really gained full support from the region's leadership. Instead, the idea to make downtown a shopping destination won out. For better or worse, financial support was given to department stores, hotel developments, and a convention center in the central business district. In 1981, $6 million were used to bring a 500-room Hyatt Regency hotel near the expanded convention center. Despite such significant investment, interviewees described disappointing outcomes. A local business executive told of the many ways in which these investments came up short.

> We maintain the fiction that we still are a downtown shopping destination. In retrospect, [I think] we spent too much time . . . trying to continue to be the downtown shopping destination and ignoring the reality of suburban shopping centers. We spent a lot of our public money subsidizing money in the Urban Development funds and all the rest, trying to make department stores work and trying to make downtown malls work.

In the end, a lot of time, energy and money were invested in downtown development and comparatively little was invested in responding to changes in the broader economy. In some ways, the early economic development response in Cincinnati actually looks more like a non-response than any sort of conscious decision; local leaders were not all that concerned with retaining heavy industry or creating a business-friendly environment. To the extent that they actively pursued any strategy at all, Cincinnati leaders eventually seemed concerned with stewarding the newer, high-tech firms of the late twentieth century. During the early 1980s, local leaders, including a 25-member Cincinnati Business Committee, made a relatively modest attempt to craft a vision for how this adaptation might unfold (LaBotz 2008). The former mayor described this effort.

> I got some funding for a weekend conference out of town, 30 miles up the way in a place called Kings Island in the dead of winter. We had 100 people . . . representing a cross-section of the community. From Friday night until Sunday, we doodled about what's good, what's bad, and what do we need to do. What are our goals and so forth. Some of the business-types that I asked to help fund this were very weary . . . In any event, we had some ideological cross-section too. People talked about racism, employment, and healthcare. At the end of the two days we also said, we need to talk about economic development because without economic development, we can't drive all the rest of it . . .

Though fairly little came of the event in terms of policy change or collective decision making, the mayor later described how the meeting helped in other ways.

> It was important that we had everyone in the room. Though I was disappointed that we weren't entirely effective, we did build up some goodwill . . . And that was really helpful for us down the road as we tried to take advantage of our machine-tool industry and the changes that were taking place in that area. We could see ourselves as a place for high-tech evolution of machine tools . . .

Ultimately, Cincinnati did see an uptick in high-technology industries and a host of 'good outcomes,' which suggest that it weathered the storm of economic restructuring comparatively well. Some of its good fortune likely relates to the fact that it was not as dependent on heavy industry as many of the other Midwestern regions were. It likely also benefited from the diverse industrial base that it had come to rely on. In his analysis of "Who Rules Cincinnati?" Dan LaBotz (2008) contends that seven corporations have long dominated Cincinnati politics, economy, and social life. These corporations include: Procter and Gamble, Kroger, Federated Department Stores (Macy's), Fifth Third Bancorp, Western and Southern Financial, American Financial Corp., and E.W. Scripps. Their strength and diversity speak volumes about the rather broad economic base that exists within the Cincinnati region.

In the end, we can surmise that the Cincinnati response to the challenges of the late 1970s and early 1980s was to somewhat passively focus on diversification. Rather than focus specifically on subsidizing business or attracting heavy industry, city and regional leaders chose to focus on cultivating the region's diverse economic base and redeveloping downtown. Most researchers would probably say that doing so paid off for the region because even when the downtown development strategies failed, the region as a whole continued to prosper.

Pittsburgh

As was the case in many other Midwestern regions, economic restructuring in the 1970s and 1980s proved extremely challenging for Pittsburgh leaders. What makes the Pittsburgh case slightly different from other regions, however, is the extent to which the region utilized public-private partnerships (Jo 2002). More specifically, the region moved away from the corporatist-governing model – influenced largely by the Allegheny Conference on Community Development – to a more inclusive public-private partnership style of governance. The new partnership included local and regional non-profits, universities, foundations, and other community-based organizations. The partnership was largely brought about by neighborhood-level challenges to the democratic machine, the conference, and their collective disproportionate focus on downtown development (Detrick 1999). The new partnership coincided largely with the beginning of Mayor Richard Caliguiri's tenure and Pittsburgh's Renaissance II period, a follow-up downtown redevelopment strategy based loosely on the earlier Renaissance I plan that unfolded during the 1940s and 1950s. Whereas Renaissance I "prevented Pittsburgh from becoming one of the problem cities of the 1960s by escaping the dire consequences of urban decline that befell such cities as Gary and Newark," Renaissance II took a different approach. During this period, the city and its mayor assumed a more managerial role, acting as development facilitator for a more regional and more inclusive group of civic and business leaders (Jacobs 2000, 89–90).

It was during the Renaissance II time period, the late 1970s and early 1980s, that Pittsburgh saw marked changes in the regional economy. Jobs were beginning to disappear from most sectors, the unemployment rate was on the rise, and various manufacturing plants closed their doors for good (Clark 1989, 47). Looking back on that period and on the economic landscape of Pittsburgh during that time, there were warning signs. A former local politician who worked in Allegheny County said that,

> In the late 1970s, the impending disaster was certainly apparent to anyone who wanted to think about it because we were far too dependent on heavy industry and becoming increasingly uncompetitive in those industries like steel, glass, and aluminum.

His concern highlights the growing need to diversify the Pittsburgh economy, an idea that was not easily accepted at that point in time. Interviewees suggested that much of the general public either did not believe the predictions of the manufacturing sector's demise or did not agree with the diversification strategies that were being proposed. One prominent businessman said that,

> At the community level there was a lot of conflict, a lot of disbelief that steel would ever disappear, because you were talking about decades and generations of families that had relied on these jobs in the industrial base. You look at these giant factories and you think, no one is ever going to disinvest in that.

At the same time, however, a small but growing number of concerned Pittsburgh residents and leaders began to lose faith. A public official working in Governor Thornburgh's office during this time period noted that,

> People were worried. Not the general public, but folks that were really looking at the economy were saying that we were too dependent on an industrial base that just isn't going to be there decades from now . . . It was very apparent by the late 1970s, and really came home to roost in the early 1980s.

As Pittsburgh grappled with the realities of economic restructuring in the late 1970s and early 1980s, pointed efforts to facilitate a stronger and more diverse economy were observed. Interviewees noted that such efforts were planned as part of a larger strategy to move the region as a whole towards recovery. Specifically, recovery strategies included a regional collaboration and later a plan for development, known as Strategy 21. Strategy 21 began in 1985 as a partnership between the City of Pittsburgh, Allegheny County, Allegheny Conference on Community Development (ACCD), Carnegie Mellon University, and the University of Pittsburgh. A 1990 plan that stemmed from this collaboration described the partnership as a "collective effort to think strategically about the directions that our region's quality of life and economy are taking, and to implement the projects and programs that are most needed to help our communities adapt to the next century" (ACCD 1990, 1). An economic development official described the process behind the creation of this regional effort.

> The Mayor and County Commissioners, along with business leaders, and the two universities, put together in 1985, a plan called Strategy 21. They came to the state for major redevelopment assistance around a new airport, industrial site redevelopment, and so on. Basically, physical investment trumped education or workforce development. That's evidence, if you will, that there was recognition that we had problems in this region and public and private sector entities had to respond.

One of the major forces behind the creation of Strategy 21 was the ACCD. Though not considered the most inclusive of organizations, the ACCD was a powerful group that carried a lot of clout in the region. The ACCD originally formed in the 1940s as an effort to coordinate regional transportation and environmental efforts. By the 1970s and 1980s, this private sector leadership organization grew more concerned with the region's economic future. Its concern led the ACCD to help create Strategy 21. As part of the Strategy 21 team, the ACCD spearheaded efforts to bolster the urban core, develop the new Pittsburgh International Airport, and found the Andy Warhol Museum. Such efforts were seen as a move towards a broader and more regional vision of the future.

Interviewees noted that, in general, Pittsburgh leaders were focused on diversifying their industrial base rather than committing solely to the revitalization of the manufacturing sector. Though leaders did not turn their backs completely on the steel industry, in the 1980s they did place much more emphasis on development strategies geared towards education, research and development, insurance, and financial services. More specifically, strategies described by interviewees and indicated in plans from this time period suggest that the Pittsburgh region was heavily prioritizing the development of new and emerging industries.

Personal reactions to the substantial losses seen in the early 1980s differed, but generally speaking there was growing support for an alternative industrial structure. A native of Pittsburgh and former member of Governor Thornburgh's cabinet described the decision to change course.

> There is literally a cliff in 1982. And we fell off it. In some sense, people like Thornburgh could see that coming. That's why, at the state level, we were working around advanced technology strategies based on the idea that we had all these technical and knowledge strengths . . . We developed the Ben Franklin Partnership as an initiative to . . . take advantage of our R&D and our research universities in order to begin developing technology- and knowledge-based jobs . . . This was the first partnership of that kind and it became a model that persists to this day.

Along with a non-profit called Innovation Works, which brought local universities together to receive state aid and other infusions of capital, the Partnership's efforts indicated a strong commitment to the diversification of the economy, which had long been over-reliant on the steel industry. Indeed, the industrial mix in Pittsburgh became far more diverse over the course of the 1970s and 1980s as the region looked towards education, healthcare, and high-technology as future growth areas (Sbragia 1990). While efforts to diversify the economy have largely proved successful, the overall employment outlook was not always so positive. For example, the number of jobs in the region has not grown in the past few decades. A former Executive Director of the Allegheny Conference described the tension between diversification and overall job creation.

> I think when people look at the overall economy, they say our employment hasn't grown and that's fair enough. But what has changed substantially is the mix in the employment base. We don't have any one employer that's big enough to cause that drop that we experienced in the early 1980s.

Though Table 4.3 indicates a mixture of both good and bad outcomes for Pittsburgh, interviewees suggested that the diversification approach was still generally beneficial to the Pittsburgh region. As in any place experiencing industrial decline, the growing pains were significant. Overall, however, the Pittsburgh region adapted comparatively well to the challenges of the late 1970s and 1980s. It is important to note, however, that in the 1990s regional employment began to fall behind the national average. Detrick (1999) suggests that this is due in part to a regional trend towards the old top-down, corporate- based planning process that was so prevalent in 1950s and 1960s Pittsburgh.

Indianapolis

Indianapolis, somewhat surprisingly, was a hotspot for automobile production in the early twentieth century. Though that sector would fade to oblivion in the 1930s, it does help to explain the hidden but substantial manufacturing roots of the Indianapolis region. Despite being one of the more geographically peripheral Rust Belt regions of this study, the Indianapolis metropolitan region of the early 1980s looked a lot more like other Midwestern regions than one might expect. In fact, manufacturing had always made up a significant portion of the region's economic base; along with healthcare, software, and telecommunications, the Indianapolis region placed great emphasis on the retention of firms related to industrial automation, instrumentation and test equipment, and consumer electronics during the 1970s (Hudnut 1995, 77). Despite the strategy initially looking a lot like one to 'Bet on the Basics' (Markusen and Carlson 1988), regional leaders ultimately shifted gears enough that the region would actually be defined by its economic diversification efforts. Before we begin any discussion of this important transition, it's first necessary to take a step back and examine the unique features of the Indianapolis region.

One of the characteristics that makes the Indianapolis case so interesting is the existence of Unigov, the consolidated city-county government that represents the City of Indianapolis and Marion County. The movement to create Unigov began in the late 1960s, when Mayor Richard Lugar developed a plan to reduce duplication in services between the city and county governments. Unigov was created on January 1, 1970 by an act of the Indiana state legislature that allowed Indianapolis to expand its boundaries so that it encompassed the majority of Marion County. This expansion allowed for the elimination of many duplicated services and created the City-County Council. Though Unigov is not generally considered a uniform success, a 1995 study suggested that it did enhance the effectiveness of economic development strategies involving public subsidization for private development (Blomquist and Parks 1995). Additionally, and perhaps more importantly, the mere existence of Unigov suggests that the region is not averse to innovative or more regional approaches to government. Even though Unigov does not represent a truly regional approach to governance – many of the suburban communities and counties are noticeably excluded – the merging of these two entities indicates a propensity to look for solutions beyond the urban core.

Further supporting this interest in a broader agenda was a regional non-aggression pact that most of the local governments agreed to. One former mayor of a suburban community noted that,

> There wasn't a whole lot being done as a region. But one thing we did do was sign a non-aggression pact, whereby we said we would not try to cannibalize your prospect just so we can get the tax base in our city. The problem is that so many cities chase rateables, chase tax bases . . . So we signed an agreement with Unigov and many neighboring suburbs saying that, "If you've got an ED [economic development] prospect, we aren't going to try and raid it and jack up the sweeteners just so we can get it and you don't. We are going to respect each other to promote ED for the whole of the region."

Such an arrangement undoubtedly played an important role in deciding how to respond to the stresses seen as a result of industrial restructuring in the late 1970s and early 1980s. As the region grappled with losses in manufacturing, leaders began to look to other industries for economic growth. Attraction strategies were an influential component of this transition in terms of economic development response. Knowing that this non-aggression pact would prevent inter-regional competition allowed for a more regional response to economic restructuring.

The story of economic restructuring in Indianapolis is an interesting one. As one former mayor of Indianapolis noted, the automobile industry had been an important part of the industrial base in the mid-twentieth century. In 1913, Indianapolis ranked second in the United States in automobile production. Since then, however, the industrial base has become highly diversified.

> We were pretty sanguine about the economic situation. We understood the importance of diversity. We had started as an automobile town. And then, because of the bankers' hardening of the arteries, the auto companies moved to Detroit. By the 1970s we were pretty well diversified.

Though it might not have felt like it at the time, an Indianapolis businessman noted that this 'hardening of the arteries' might have been a blessing in disguise.

> When the auto jobs began to leave town, we knew that we had to do something. In fact, even before they officially left, we had reason to believe that these shops weren't going to stay around forever. We didn't ignore this bad news. Instead, we tried to figure out other ways for Indianapolis to get ahead. Now, we know that we were lucky. We really dodged a bullet.

Avoiding the plight of other over-specialized Midwestern regions, public sector leaders in the Indianapolis region took early and swift actions to diversify their economy and move towards reorganization. Rather than clinging to automobile manufacturing or the other heavy industries that had been mainstays in the past, Indianapolis leaders chose to reorganize the regional economy by emphasizing business attraction, indigenous entrepreneurship, and sports-based tourism development strategies.

While the business attraction and entrepreneurship approaches were certainly useful to the Indianapolis economy, it is the sports-based development for which the region is best known. A former economic development specialist for Unigov pointed out that "We embarked on this sports strategy not as an end in itself but as a means to an end of economic development." In other words, the cultivation of sports-based development in Indianapolis was designed to complement the regional economy, rather than be the foundation on which everything else rested. Important components of this approach include the successful attraction of the Indianapolis Colts National Football League team from Baltimore and continued loyalty of the National Basketball Association's Indiana Pacers, the construction of a downtown stadium and convention center, and the expansion of the Indianapolis Motor Speedway, which is home to the Indianapolis 500. As one former mayor notes, such moves were highly strategic.

> When we built the downtown stadium, it was the first time in the country that a stadium had been yoked into a convention center. And our determination was that we weren't going to build this out in a cornfield somewhere so that they can only play 12 days a year. We're going to make this an asset with a convention center . . . When the Colts finally came in 1984 that was icing on the cake. That was nice for me because politically there was a hell of a lot of risk building a big stadium that seats 62,000 people . . . without a team to play there. After it was announced that the Colts were coming, downtown really perked up again.

To be certain, the sports-based approach has resulted in substantial gains for the Indianapolis region. A 1994 study found that Indianapolis is a unique case in that it was the only American city where the presence of professional sports teams exerted a "statistically significant, positive impact on the metro area economy" (Baade 1994, 19). Baade (1994) attributes the positive impact to a combination of things, including the statewide tradition of sports involvement, the relatively small size of the region, and the "city's commitment to defining itself as America's sports capital, particularly for amateur sports" (Ibid., 19).

As these formidable investments imply, capturing the tourism and convention market was an *active* strategy pursued by city and regional leadership in the 1970s and 1980s. As Swindell et al. (1995) suggest, "The city's leadership had decided to change the image of Indianapolis through an extensive amateur sports emphasis that was joined with a downtown revitalization program. Together, sports and a new downtown were going to change Indianapolis's image and improve economic development" (143). Building on the nearly century-long success of the Indianapolis 500, the region has actively transitioned to become a sports destination for events like the Super Bowl, NCAA Basketball Final Four, and regular games for the Colts and the Pacers, among others. Attracting conventions has also been another regional strategy put forth by local leaders. The Indianapolis region has also played host to numerous meetings including the Future Farmers of America and Gen Con, a role-playing game convention.

Nevertheless, the sports-based development strategy has not been foolproof, especially in the long run. Numerous interviewees described today's Indianapolis as a region experiencing pronounced challenges. A former Marion County economic development official noted that many of the problems that had been avoided in the past are now beginning to rear their ugly heads.

> I think we are now struggling to maintain the core . . . The problem is the people who have been moving to the suburbs, they suck the vitality out. We aren't as bad as Pittsburgh is. But throughout the Rust Belt, you've got that same problem of people leaving. Whether or not they are going to return or if there is going to be an influx of new people, remains to be seen . . . the wealth and the power was moving out to the wealthier, cleaner suburbs . . . What can we do to keep people in town? I think we need to improve amenities and city services . . . It's a never-ending fight for urban America to compete with the suburban dream.

Like so many other Midwestern regions, the Indianapolis regional economy continues to struggle today. In this case, however, the problem is less about the region's economic legacy than it is about classic centrifugal forces pulling people and jobs outward. When compared to other Midwestern regions, Indianapolis has experienced a fair amount of success. Whether or not this success would have occurred even without the region's unique approach to economic development is impossible to know. Nevertheless, it seems that the Indianapolis leaders' conscious decision to adapt by moving away from manufacturing and towards a more diverse economic base likely played a prominent role in determining this region's comparatively healthy economic path.

Columbus

In its early years, the Columbus region was settled largely by German and Irish immigrants. By the early nineteenth century, those who came to Columbus generally found a relatively stable and liberal community with an economy rooted in transportation, brewing, and, by the late 1840s, railroads. Because of its location at various inland crossroads, the Columbus region emerged as a major transportation nexus. As one former planning official noted, this strategic inland position affected the regional economy in a variety of ways.

> Having five railroads here led to a transportation and foodstuffs-oriented economy . . . We had various rail yards, supply organizations and steel equipment, not steel mills but people who use steel and make it into things . . . We also did a lot of defense industry production but I guess we had a lot less of the heavy industry than most other Midwestern cities.

For much of the late nineteenth century and early twentieth century, the Columbus regional economy flourished as goods and people moved through the region. During World War II, the region played a large role in the production of naval defense equipment. As such, economic prosperity continued largely uninterrupted into the early post-war years. However, as defense production slowed following World War II, the region was forced to consider its next course of action. As a local land-use attorney described, a number of crucial decisions were made during this time period.

> The goal of the city administration, basically Mayor Jack Sensenbrenner, in the early 1960s was to figure out how to build a strong economic base without relying on heavy industry. Heavy industry . . . was not encouraged to be here. And that decision led to increasing support for the education network (we've got 11 universities within 30 miles), a major number of insurance companies here (Nationwide being the largest), and we had a lot of large banks until they started collapsing into various things . . .

Columbus is a region in which the leadership proactively and publicly adapted to deindustrialization by moving away from heavy industry. In a sense, the Columbus region moved to diversify its base before deindustrialization really even took hold in the Midwest. Though manufacturing never had the presence in Columbus that it did in other Midwestern regions – manufacturing as a percent of total employment was the lowest here of all eight regions – it still fueled significant portions of the region's early economy. Other early industrial strengths included steel processing and carriage production. As the state capital and home to the Ohio State University, the region's economy has also benefited from the relatively stable employment base provided by government and the university.

Over the course of the 1970s, Sensenbrenner's earlier-laid plans began to take shape, and the Columbus economic base gradually shifted to an economy based less on manufacturing and heavy industry and more on transportation, the movement of goods, and the production and distribution of clothing. One local businessman describes what this has meant for the region.

> We have become, recognizing that Columbus is in close proximity to much of the US population, a transportation-oriented distribution center for retail goods, money, insurance, and education, all of which were in line with the original goals of Jack Sensenbrenner. Consequently, it has given us a pretty stable, non-boom and bust economy.

One of the main private sector players in this transition was Les Wexner, founder of The Limited Brands clothing company. A Columbus historian described Wexner's progression from startup to multinational corporation.

> In the late 1960s, a dreamer called Les Wexner started a woman's clothing store . . . The Limited Brands . . . As Wexner expanded into different apparel lines – and needed a huge supply of inventory – he created a distribution system tied to cargo places from Southeast Asia. This then created, in the 1980s, a major distribution warehousing operation, not heavy industry at all . . . Everything coming in that was needed in their stores, was repackaged and sent out by container to each of the particular stores in the chain, nationally.

The Limited Brands today represents a very important and expansive component of the Columbus economy. In the last few decades, the corporation has either bought or started numerous other retail brands, all of which have their headquarters in Columbus. They include: Victoria's Secret, Pink, Bath and Body Works, C.O. Bigelow, White Barn Candle Company, and others. Other important clothing-related corporations also call Columbus home, including Hollister and Abercrombie and Fitch, as well as Retail Ventures, which is responsible for DSW, Filene's Basement, and Value City stores. Together, these clothing and retail companies make up a substantial portion of the economy and have played an important role in its diversification. Other notable corporations in the area include Wendy's (fast food restaurant chain), Chemical Abstracts Corporation (scientific information), and Worthington Industries (steel processing).

When asked what factors may have played a role in the relative success of the Columbus region, interviewees commonly mentioned two main factors: a policy of liberal annexation of surrounding land and an invested group of Columbus-area leaders. The move towards annexation began under the reign of Mayor Sensenbrenner, who wanted to avoid the landlocked fate of other Ohio cities. Beginning in the 1950s, Sensenbrenner used water as leverage; any developers outside of the city that desired water and utilities would have to annex their land either into the city or into a suburb whose service area was controlled by Columbus (Jacobs 1998). This policy protected the city's tax base from the rampant suburbanization seen during this time period. One local developer described how this annexation policy strengthened the region and allowed leaders to control development within its boundaries.

> Sensenbrenner . . . had a policy of annexing anything. We'll extend infrastructure out to it and build so that Columbus does not become surrounded by suburbs as in the case of Cleveland, Cincinnati, and Buffalo for that matter. In all of those instances, those urban cores were isolated by suburbia . . . The annexation policy was exceedingly successful and precluded Columbus from being surrounded, which meant it was able to capture the income tax base and control the type of development in Central Ohio.

Overall, the annexation policy has proven relatively successful. The city has increased its total land from 39 square miles at the beginning of annexation to 210 square miles today. This increase in land has brought an increase in both tax base and population. However, the playing field is not always even for those who live within city limits. Since the mid-1970s, people living in newly annexed areas have been allowed to send their children to suburban schools, thereby reaping the benefits of being within city limits but avoiding the struggling Columbus Public School District. As one would expect, this policy has had a considerable effect on the region's housing landscape. As Jacobs (1998) noted, "between 1980 and 1990, the total number of housing units inside the Columbus Public School District actually dropped 2.1 percent; during the same span, aggregate housing units in the City of Columbus increased 17.5 percent" (136). Population trends from this time period indicate a similar fate. Together, these numbers hint at the potential downside of Sensenbrenner's decisions and suggest that while the policy may have been good for the region's tax base, it was less beneficial in terms of regional equity. Though Sensenbrenner was a powerful mayor, the annexation policy and numerous other policies, plans, and strategies would never have been possible without the backing of a regional leadership group known as the Titans. This powerful group of civic leaders was highly influential in the decision-making process during the deindustrialization period and beyond. As one local historian and Columbus resident noted, this group shaped the region's trajectory in a variety of ways.

> The leadership condition downtown at that point, was primarily the local utilities, the major commercial retail interests, Nationwide and the other insurance companies, Wolf Industries, which is the media conglomerate . . . and then the banks. All of those men knew each other well. Their biggest arguments were about how badly Ohio State was going to beat Michigan. You had a lot of people cooperatively working together and Sensenbrenner was closely involved with that. They were known as the Titans. It wasn't necessarily a fixed group; you just sort of knew something was happening. They were the ones that made the plan and then marketed it. Their ultimate goal was a strong, diversified and stable economy.

Little exists in the way of formal documentation of the Titans' work but interviewees agreed that the group had a lot of power over the development decisions made during the latter half of the twentieth century.

Like in so many other regions, Columbus leaders must have been concerned with creating a good economic climate for their own businesses. However, their overall approach to regional economic development was slightly different than most other places because it was preemptive rather than reactive and also actively prioritized a diverse economic base. Though it is impossible to determine whether the Columbus region's comparative success and abundance of 'good outcomes' was a result of having chosen this particular approach or just of the preemptive manner in which it was applied, it does offer us important insight into one region's unique response or *pre-response* to deindustrialization.

Conclusions

As the four regions in this chapter attest, there was more than one way for regional leaders to approach a move away from manufacturing.

Though all would eventually move towards some type of diversification in their economic base, the four regions – Cincinnati, Pittsburgh, Indianapolis, and Columbus – all designed and then followed different paths on their way to recovery. Both the variations and similarities seen in their pathways offer lessons for regions facing longer-term stresses like deindustrialization.

Common regional characteristics

In the four regions where decisions were made to move away from manufacturing, the most popular course of action was to diversify their economic bases through new business formation or by attracting businesses from elsewhere. In Indianapolis, regional leaders started with an emphasis on manufacturing but gradually shifted towards a diversification and sports-based strategy over time. In Cincinnati, Columbus, and Pittsburgh, diversification was pursued almost exclusively. However, it should be noted that though all four regions pursued diversification, the degree to which they consciously engaged in this type of adaptive response varied significantly. For instance, in Columbus, regional leaders actively pursued a strategy of diversification and a shift away from manufacturing. In Cincinnati, on the other hand, leaders effectively chose non-response, acting as stewards of the new economy rather than advocates of any major economic development agenda.

Another commonality across most of these regions can be seen in the easy identification of a single leader or leadership group responsible for economic development decisions in the 1970s and 1980s. Indianapolis's Mayor William Hudnut was a central player in that region's shift to a tourism- and sports-based development strategy. In Columbus, two leadership entities combined to make the important decisions: Mayor Jack Sensenbrenner in the late 1960s and early 1970s, and the Titans thereafter. And in Pittsburgh, many of the important decisions came from Mayor Richard Caliguiri and the ACCD. Cincinnati's leadership was less defined, which makes sense, given the non-response we saw there. In all but one of these regions, there was an easily identifiable leader, or as Mayor Hudnut would say, "someone in charge of minding the store." Distinctive leadership played a very important role in taking stock of the region's assets and opportunities, gathering input from other local leaders and confidants, acting as liaisons between local, state, and federal entities, and ultimately deciding how each region would pursue its own economic development strategy.

In general, these four regions that chose to diversify were less dependent on manufacturing than their counterparts, who chose instead to bet on manufacturing. Recall from Chapter 4 that Buffalo, Cleveland, Detroit, and Milwaukee had a larger percent of jobs in manufacturing to begin with. Though such figures provide little evidence in the way of causation, the association between lower levels of manufacturing and the decision to concentrate on economic development strategies outside of traditional manufacturing suggests that further study of this correlation is warranted.

Lessons learned

Moving beyond commonalities and towards lessons we might draw from these four regions, two main points emerge. First, these histories suggest that among those regions that chose to actively diversify, *the regions that responded earlier to the unfolding challenges of deindustrialization were more likely to experience 'good outcomes' in the long run.* The benefits of an early response seem especially relevant in the cases of Columbus and Indianapolis, though their individual experiences differed greatly. In the case of Columbus, interviewees noted an early and conscious decision to move away from manufacturing as early as the 1960s. Though we do not know whether this decision was pure luck or the result of serious deliberations and calculated projections, further exploration along those lines would be a useful line of questioning for future research. In the case of Indianapolis, the decision to diversify was not as easy or as early as it was in Columbus. The Indianapolis region tried first to shore up its manufacturing base but was discouraged by the results. Leaders then shifted towards diversification strategies, emphasizing tourism- and sports-based development strategies as a way of differentiating themselves from other Midwestern industrial regions. Despite the early emphasis on manufacturing, the region still made moves toward a diversification approach in the early 1970s, long before many of the other regions even acknowledged that they had an impending problem. Once decided upon, the move away from manufacturing and towards alternative industries was deliberate and swift in both regions. Though the long-term benefits of this response are difficult to isolate from other potential reasons for their relative success, the relationship between the timing of a region's response and 'good outcomes' is certainly worth further exploration.

The second important finding from these regions is that *innovative approaches – whether they worked or not – were almost always a part of the diversification process.* Creative approaches to dealing with the problems of deindustrialization allowed many of these regions to ostensibly 'turn the corner' by reinventing themselves or by leveraging their assets in new ways. Unlike many of the regions that chose to 'Bet on the Basics' by committing to a recreation of the past, many of the regional leaders discussed in this chapter were much more inventive when devising an economic development plan to 'Bow Out' and move their region towards recovery.

As we saw above, the Indianapolis region analyzed its strengths and weaknesses, looked for an angle in which it might do well, and ultimately decided to build a new (and risky) downtown stadium as one major step towards its sports-based response. In Cincinnati, regional leaders took a gamble on downtown living and shopping; though this would not bode well for the region in the long run, it was still a relatively innovative approach at that point in time.

Columbus leaders hedged their bets by adopting a policy of liberal annexation of surrounding lands to ensure that suburbanization did not engulf the region.[1] And finally, leaders in Pittsburgh devised Strategy 21, a plan that prioritized physical investment over things like education or workforce development. By all means this was a risky plan, but it was generally considered a success in that it targeted specific forms of development and asked other regional actors to help provide supplemental support. To the extent that such creativity is related to the flexibility of a region, the innovative responses associated with diversification might also relate to higher levels of adaptive resilience in these regions. The ability to bend, adapt, and come up with creative solutions to insidious problems is likely an important characteristic of adaptive resilience.

Overall, what we learn from further examination of these regions, and the leaders interviewed in each, is that the gambles taken in Indianapolis, Cincinnati, Columbus, and Pittsburgh all played out in different ways. Some regions gracefully turned the metaphorical 'corner' and found a new economic mix or focus, while others found it difficult to navigate deindustrialization's uncharted waters. Though all four regions would ultimately diversify, no two regions did so in the same way.

Note

1 Although Milwaukee also utilized annexation, the Columbus region annexed land for residential, commercial, and industrial development, whereas Milwaukee primarily annexed land for industrial development, which was more difficult and reinforced Milwaukee's 'Betting on the Basics' approach.

References

Allegheny Conference on Community Development (ACCD). 1990. *Strategy 21: Competing in a World Economy – Environment, Access, Jobs, Advanced Technology*. Pittsburgh, PA.

Baade, Robert A. 1994. "Stadiums, Professional Sports, and Economic Development: Assessing the Reality." *Heartland Policy Study* 28(62): 1–39.

Blomquist, William, and Roger B. Parks. 1995. "Fiscal, Service, and Political Impacts of Indianapolis-Marion County's Unigov." *The Journal of Federalism* 25(4): 37–54.

Clark, Gordon. 1989. "Pittsburgh in Transition: Consolidation of Prosperity in an Era of Economic Restructuring." In *Economic Restructuring and Political Response*, edited by Robert Beauregard, 41–69. Newbury Park: Sage Press.

Detrick, Sabina. 1999. "The Post Industrial Revitalization of Pittsburgh: Myths and Evidence." *Journal of Planning Literature* 34(1): 4–12.

Hudnut, William H. 1995. *The Hudnut Years in Indianapolis 1976–1991*. Indianapolis, IN: Indiana University Press.

Jacobs, Brian. 2000. *Strategy and Partnerships in Cities and Regions: Economic Development and Urban Regeneration in Pittsburgh, Birmingham and Rotterdam*. New York: St. Martin's Press.

Jacobs, Gregory. 1998. *Getting Around Brown: Desegregation, Development, and the Columbus Public Schools*. Columbus, OH: Ohio State University Press.

Jo, Hyung Je. 2002. "Regional Restructuring and Urban Regimes: A Comparison of the Pittsburgh and Detroit Metropolitan Areas." Office for the Study of Automotive Transportation. University of Michigan Transportation Research Institute, UMTRI 2002–20.

LaBotz, Dan. 2008. "Who Rules Cincinnati? A Study of Cincinnati's Economic Power Structure and its Impact on Communities and People." Accessed January 30, 2012. www.CincinnatiStudies.org.

Markusen, Ann, and Virginia Carlson. 1988. "Bowing Out, Bidding Down, and Betting on the Basics: Midwestern Responses to Deindustrialization in the 1980s." Center for Urban Affairs and Policy Research, Working Paper, Northeastern University, Boston, MA.

Sbragia, Alberta. 1990. "Pittsburgh's 'Third Way': The Nonprofit Sector as a Key to Urban Regeneration." In *Leadership and Urban Regeneration: Cities in North American and Europe* edited by Dennis Judd and Michael Parkinson, 51–68. London, UK: Sage.

Spring, Joel. 1984. "The Structure of Power in an Urban School System: A Study of Cincinnati School Politics." *Curriculum Inquiry* 14(4): 401–424.

Stradling, David. 2003. *Cincinnati, Ohio: From River City to Highway Metropolis*. Chicago, IL: Arcadia.

Swindell, David W., Mark S. Rosentraub, Daniel R. Mullins, and Michael Przybylski. 1995. "The Amateur Sports Strategy." In *The Hudnut Years in Indianapolis: 1976–1991*, edited by William Hudnut, 143–152. Bloomington, IN: Indiana University Press.

7 Conclusion

The art of adaptive resilience

From the interviews and subsequent analyses emerge a plethora of important findings about the types of responses seen in these eight regions. Table 7.1 highlights the significant variation seen across regions in terms of response type and specific strategies. A quick tally of the case study regions suggests that 'Bowing Out' and 'Betting on the Basics' were the most often utilized response types during this time period. In other words, the most popular approach amongst these large Rust Belt regions was to either 'fight or take flight.' Leaders in these Rust Belt regions either 'fought' against deindustrialization by continuing to target existing heavy industry for economic development initiatives or 'fled' by abandoning the struggling manufacturing sector and focusing on other industrial sectors for development. Though elements of 'Bidding Down' and 'Sharing the Wealth' were seen in some of the case study regions, regional actors were far more likely to use 'Bowing Out' or 'Betting on the Basics' as an over-arching guide to their respective economic development responses.

To help us understand how these decisions relate to adaptive resilience, we will revisit the hypotheses first mentioned in Chapter 4. Final thoughts on remaining questions and future research opportunities are then discussed. Longer-term implications in light of the Great Recession close out this chapter and the book.

Revisiting hypothesis 1: diversity of the decision-making body

Turning to measures of performance, using both quantitative and qualitative data, we see subtle, but important, variation across cases. Recall that the first hypothesis proposed in Chapter 4 predicted that *regions with a diverse and broadly representative decision-making body would be more likely to exhibit adaptive resilience and experience 'good outcomes.'* In other words, we would expect such regions to better navigate the economic uncertainties associated with deindustrialization and turn the metaphorical 'corner' by bringing together a diverse coalition of economic development actors. Alternatively, we might expect to see less evidence of adaptive resilience in

Table 7.1 Selected characteristics of regional responses to deindustrialization

Region	*Response type*	*Notable characteristics of regional response*
Buffalo	Betting on the Basics	• Labor/management conflicts • Retention focus
Cincinnati	Bowing Out	• Passive diversification • Downtown development
Cleveland	Betting on the Basics	• Political progressivism • Land bank • Emphasis on equity
Columbus	Bowing Out	• Early diversification • Transportation, clothing production and distribution • Annexation
Detroit	Betting on the Basics	• Committed to automobile • Workforce development • Fragmented region
Indianapolis	Bowing Out	• Unigov • Non-aggression pact • Sports-based tourism • Active diversification
Milwaukee	Betting on the Basics	• High-tech manufacturing • Annexation and land banking • Workforce development
Pittsburgh	Bowing Out	• Diversification • Focus on new and emerging industries • Public-private partnerships

regions where unilateral decisions were made or in places where one sector of leadership wielded the majority of the decision-making power.

The qualitative case studies in Chapters 5 and 6 reveal substantial differences in the composition of economic development decision-making bodies between the 'Basic Betters' and those who 'Bowed Out.' Amongst the 'Basic Betters,' we generally see a lack of diversity in terms of who was involved in the decision-making process. In Buffalo and Milwaukee, a largely public sector response to deindustrialization was observed, while a more private sector orientation was detected in Detroit and Cleveland. Mayor Griffin and other city officials made most of the early economic development decisions in Buffalo. Though that public sector orientation would skew towards the private sector with the arrival of the Gang of 18 later on, early decisions in the Buffalo region were primarily made in City Hall or by the Erie County Industrial Development Authority. Milwaukee leaders largely aligned with Mayor Maier's agenda, which was to use annexed land for industrial land-banking purposes. Land banking for the purposes of economic development occurred in both the city and in the suburbs and generally occurred on land that had been purchased, cleared, and subsequently 'banked' by the public sector. Private sector leadership likely played a role in other economic development decisions but not nearly as much as it did in other regions like Columbus or Cincinnati.

The responses seen in Detroit and Cleveland by no means excluded the public sector, but the composition and orientation of their stakeholder groups differed slightly from those of Buffalo and Milwaukee. There was some variety in terms of the actors involved in economic development decisions in Detroit, but the most vocal actors tended to be public officials with close ties to the 'Big Three.' Many in the public sector supported a pro-business agenda, which facilitated a de facto corporatist-governing model. In Cleveland, early decisions about how to respond came from the public sector, but also from the Cleveland Foundation-funded study on Cleveland's metropolitan economy. Findings from the study largely focused on supporting existing strengths in durable goods manufacturing, with comparatively less interest in developing new specialties in technologically advanced industries. Leaders in Cleveland City Hall eventually proposed equity-focused strategies, but, as was mentioned in Chapter 5, few of these ideas actually translated into economic development policy changes. In the end, both Detroit and Cleveland skewed more towards the private sector, but one would be hard pressed to say that they engendered diverse or broadly representative decision-making bodies.

Among the regions that 'Bowed Out,' we saw slightly more variety in terms of the actors involved in the decision-making process. Regional actors were involved in both Indianapolis's and Pittsburgh's decision-making processes. Indianapolis's well-known example of Unigov, along with its non-aggression agreements, made for a rather diverse and regionalized approach to economic development. Though the public sector, and especially Mayor Hudnut, played a large role in shaping the Indianapolis response, the overall approach was regional in nature and included a variety of actors aimed at improving the economic plight of the region. In Pittsburgh, public-private partnerships enabled redevelopment to occur after steel manufacturing began its decline. In particular, the Allegheny Conference on Community Development and the resulting Strategy 21 reflected a broad coalition of regional leaders guided primarily by Mayor Caliguiri who acted as 'development facilitator.'

Columbus and Cincinnati also brought together fairly broad economic development coalitions to deal with deindustrialization, but did so with more representation from the private sector. In Cincinnati, it was the 25-member Cincinnati Business Commission that coalesced to act on the private sector's behalf. The commission included representation from the seven main corporations that dominated Cincinnati's economy (Proctor and Gamble, Kroger, Federated Department Stores, Fifth Third Bancorp, Western and Southern Financial, American Financial Corporation, and E.W. Scripps). In Columbus, a strong government and university presence all but ensured that there would be representatives from public sector and higher education at the economic development decision-making table. In addition, a strong early vision from Mayor Sensenbrenner helped shape much of the Columbus economy. Key private sector players, along with the Titans civic leaders group, rounded out a fairly robust set of regional decision-making actors.

Although the distinction between 'Basic Betters' and those who 'Bowed Out' is not absolute, those who 'Bowed Out' tended to incorporate broader interests in their economic development decision-making process. In other words, there may be correlation between regions that incorporated a diversity of partners and those that chose to diversify their economic bases and move beyond manufacturing. While causation has not been proven, these case studies reveal that the relationship between diverse leadership and adaptive resilience is likely an important one. Economic development decisions, which are often quite costly and sometimes rather risky, ought not to be made unilaterally, nor made in a vacuum. Instead, they ideally involve a host of actors (recall the many chefs in the kitchen example) who represent an array of interests. The optimal number and variety of actors is not known, but these findings suggest that there are benefits to diversity and a multiplicity of perspectives, especially in regions that are confronting a serious challenge like deindustrialization. Such variety and insight should contribute to a more flexible and reflective response.

Revisiting hypothesis 2: commitment to manufacturing

One has to look no further than recent newspaper headlines lamenting the fiscal state of Detroit and Cleveland to deduce that regions that committed to manufacturing and 'Bet on the Basics' have experienced substantial economic challenges in the aftermath of deindustrialization. Recall that hypothesis 2 predicted a similar fate, namely that *regions in which leaders committed to manufacturing by 'Betting on the Basics' would not adapt as readily or as well as regions where leaders pursued other alternatives*. When Markusen and Carlson (1988) developed this typology, however, the authors presented an argument that was the near polar opposite of this hypothesis. At that time, the authors predicted, 'Betting on the Basics' may offer greater prospects for long-term success (1).

The quantitative data presented in Chapter 4 suggest that the four regions whose leaders chose to 'Bet on the Basics' were amongst the worst performers in both the response and recovery periods, meaning that they did not exhibit adaptive resilience, at least in terms of the quantitative data. However, if we look back to the findings from the qualitative data presented in Chapters 5 and 6, the results are mixed. In Buffalo and Detroit, the qualitative accounts suggest that these regions exhibited lower levels of adaptive resilience. Predictably, these regional economies have suffered great losses in recent decades and both continue to experience a hollowing-out of their regional population. The qualitative data on Cleveland and Milwaukee, however, paint a slightly more optimistic picture. These regions have seen modest population growth and a moderately successful transition from heavy industry to an increasingly high-tech economic base, which may be attributed to their slightly higher levels of adaptive resilience. In Cleveland, interviewees described regional improvements in terms of equity and workforce development. In Milwaukee, the region that quite literally 'Bet on the Basics,' interviewees similarly described the innovative approaches used to retain and expand manufacturing, a technique that has worked fairly well for the region in recent years. These mixed results suggest that further investigation along these lines would be a useful contribution to future research.

We move now beyond 'Betting on the Basics' to the other preeminent approach – 'Bowing Out' – which was employed in four regions: Cincinnati, Pittsburgh, Indianapolis, and Columbus. In these four regions, the general consensus of regional leadership was that the manufacturing sector's heyday was largely in the past. Regional leaders believed that heavy industry had peaked and that it was time to think about ways to 'turn the corner' and explore other options to anchor the regional economic base. 'Bowing Out' afforded regions the opportunity to pursue these other options, like transportation and clothing distribution in Columbus, sports-based tourism in Indianapolis, or consumer goods and retail trade in Cincinnati. The diversification strategy seems to have paid off for most of these regions as indicated by the 'good outcomes' seen in terms of population stabilization or growth and modest improvements in equity. In Pittsburgh, which has recently been heralded for its increasingly diverse economic base, the transition has taken slightly longer. Nonetheless, recent employment rebounds and population stabilization suggest that 'Bowing Out' has resulted in an increasingly healthy regional economy.

If we think about the figure-8 diagram used in the adaptive cycle model (Figure 2.1), we can imagine the 'Bowing Out' approach as a deliberate attempt to 'turn the corner' and move beyond the uncertainty of the reorganization phase and into the exploitation phase, a period of growth and opportunity. On the other hand, we can imagine that those regions that chose to 'Bet on the Basics' struggled against global forces to maintain the stability of the conservation phase. Unfortunately, for most of these regions, the rigidity associated with the conservation phase ultimately proved to be quite detrimental in the longer term. In a place like Detroit, which for many decades appeared to have prolonged its stability in the conservation phase, the rigidity associated with such intense specialization likely triggered the region's precipitous fall in later decades. Though the qualitative data presented in this research do not prove causation, the findings do suggest a need to further explore the association between 'turning the corner,' 'Bowing Out,' and adaptive resilience.

Revisiting hypothesis 3: early response

Further consideration should also be given to the third hypothesis proposed in Chapter 4, which stated that *adaptive resilience will be seen in regions where leaders responded to early signs of deindustrialization and quickly developed an appropriate economic development response.* Again, the results seen in the quantitative and qualitative data paint a colorful picture. However, greater adaptive resilience and better outcomes were generally associated with an early response.

In Detroit, where the response remained largely unchanged throughout the late 1970s and 1980s, there was little haste. Though most interviewees recalled early conversations about the problems facing the region, very few remember any type of early strategic plan to move the region towards recovery. For most of the time period of interest, leaders in Detroit chose a veritable non-response approach by continuing on the same trajectory, giving incentives to large automobile corporations and supporting workers where they could. Their response was not only slow, but also lacked the insight and strategy that a more successful response might have had. A similarly sluggish and lack-luster response was also seen in Buffalo, where leaders spent a lot of time and energy debating how to respond, with very little to show for it in the end. In Cleveland, the response was more organized but still quite sluggish. The region would wait until 1982 to commission the Rand report on the status of the regional economy. Although ultimately well thought out, the 'Betting on the Basics'-type response occurred a little too late. Even later (but slightly more effective) were the attempts made to 'Share the Wealth' in the Cleveland region. The delayed response in Cleveland may be explained in part by the relatively slow pace with which the region lost manufacturing jobs. Whereas other regions saw sudden drop-offs in manufacturing, Cleveland's losses took years longer to unfold.

Rounding out the regions that 'Bet on the Basics,' a slightly more expedient response was seen in Milwaukee, where regional leaders began annexing and banking land in the 1950s and 1960s for later industrial development efforts. Though some interviewees described this effort as a gamble that happened to pay off, it is undeniable that there was some amount of foresight involved in crafting this type of early response. Leaders heeded the warning that challenges loomed ahead, and implemented a plan to make the region more attractive to manufacturing firms. Milwaukee's efforts to get ahead of the curve were part of a conscious decision to use economic and industrial development tools to respond to the challenges of deindustrialization. Though the region's response and recovery resilience was not the best of the case study regions, the Milwaukee region fared relatively well – often times right around the mean – considering its disproportionately high dependence on manufacturing and its limited available attraction mechanisms. Qualitatively, the region's flexible and innovative approach to 'Betting on the Basics' suggests that it exhibited at least some elements of adaptive resilience in the face of deindustrialization; like the example of the reed in the wind, the Milwaukee region was better situated to bend rather than break during the 1970s and 1980s.

Turning now to an examination of the timing of responses seen in those regions that 'Bowed Out,' we again see rather mixed results. Among the more sluggish responders were Pittsburgh and Cincinnati. In Pittsburgh, regional leaders were slow in their response because many believed that manufacturing losses were cyclical, rather than structural. Though the region would eventually shift directions by moving towards a public-private partnership model that would ultimately encourage the region to 'Bow Out,' the response was slow and the region suffered greatly while leaders decided what to do and how to do it. In Cincinnati, non-response was the order of the day. Leaders in that region acted as stewards, rather than shapers, of the 'Bowing Out'-like response. By and large, that non-response paid off for the region; Cincinnati performed better than the mean on all of the recovery-period measures.

Though their strategies and regional outcomes varied greatly, leaders in both Indianapolis and Columbus were relatively pro-active in their response to deindustrialization. Flexibility was the hallmark of the response seen in Indianapolis. Because of very early retention efforts in that region, the regional response initially looked like 'Betting on the Basics.' However, regional leaders described how a quick and decisive change in plan during the 1970s set the region on a very different path. Responding to early losses in manufacturing, regional leaders decided to pursue a sports- and tourism-based development agenda instead. This change in approach worked fairly well for the region in the long run, largely isolating it from many of the economic challenges of the past few decades. A similar change in direction was also pursued in Columbus, albeit at a much earlier point in time. Columbus leaders, foreseeing some of the challenges associated with an overly specialized economy, opted to diversify their economy before the term deindustrialization had even been coined. In the ultimate preemptive strike, Columbus leaders began to 'Bow Out' in the early 1960s, long before most other regions in this study. Early efforts to diversify their economy appear to have paid off, as the region fairs well on most qualitative and quantitative indicators of response and recovery.

Although the exact timing could not always be pinpointed, the responses seen in the eight case study regions suggest that there is an underlying pattern. Many of the regions that responded swiftly did exhibit adaptive resilience, namely Columbus, Indianapolis, and Milwaukee. Other regions – including Buffalo, Cleveland, Detroit, and Pittsburgh – reacted less quickly, because they lacked either the wherewithal, authority, consensus, or gumption to do so. In these regions, adaptive resilience was observed but less so than in those regions that acted swiftly. And in Cincinnati, where manufacturing was slightly less important to the regional economy, non-action is the best way to describe the region's relatively successful non-response to deindustrialization.

Overall, the case studies demonstrate that regions generally are quite capable of adaptation and remind us that adaptive resilience is a useful lens through which we can examine regional responses. *The adaptive resilience concept is most useful when both quantitative and qualitative measures are incorporated; examining only one type of measure often masks some of the more subtle nuances of a given regional response.*

Remaining questions and future research

Data collected for the purposes of this research have been immensely useful in terms of identifying the different economic development approaches that regions used to respond to deindustrialization. However, like in any good research project, additional research questions have revealed themselves over the course of this exploration. Though the above research hints at some potential answers, it is beyond the scope of this study to sufficiently address these questions here. Nevertheless, these remaining questions should serve as the basis for exciting future research on regions, resilience, and deindustrialization.

One of the more interesting findings from this research is that the types of actors sitting at the decision-making table varied greatly across cases. In some regions, the public sector wielded a heavy hand in the crafting of a response. In others, the private sector called the shots. In most regions, it was a combination of public, private, and civic sector leaders that decided how to proceed. Given the sheer variety seen in terms of actors, one might be inclined to ask how certain types of decisions were made. More specifically, we might ask where the foresight to 'turn the corner' comes from. Or, why did some regions decide to 'Bow Out' while others chose to 'Bet on the Basics'? How did regional leaders in Indianapolis and Columbus foresee the need to diversify their industrial bases? Knowing more about where this insight came from, and why only some regional leaders had it, would be immensely helpful to researchers and practitioners alike.

Another question raised by this research is whether racial segregation played a role in how regions responded to deindustrialization. Amongst regions that 'Bet on the Basics,' racial segregation was quite prevalent. This begs the question of whether racial divisions within these regions affected how and how well these regions responded to the challenges of deindustrialization. Though some interviewees discussed problems of racial division and racism within their regions, their accounts were by no means conclusive. Further investigation along these lines would be helpful to researchers and practitioners alike.

If we move from demography to geography, an additional set of questions emerge. Knowing that policies of annexation featured so prominently in at least three of the case study regions, we must ask if regional geography relates to how well a region has fared in light of deindustrialization. In Detroit, Buffalo, and to some extent in Pittsburgh, being 'boxed in' by surrounding suburbs acted as a serious impediment to economic development within the urban core. Expansive, shovel-ready sites were not generally available to corporations looking to locate or expand in the central cities. On the other hand, in Milwaukee, Columbus, and, to some extent, Indianapolis there were deliberate and often aggressive policies to annex land. In most cases, this annexation helped improve chances of fiscal stability in the central city, which was the anchor in most of these regions. Whether this economic development strategy of early annexation (before it became impossible) was the reason for the slightly better outcomes in these three regions is a question that certainly merits further study.

Having discovered that adaptive resilience was more likely in those regions that chose to 'Bow Out,' it stands then that certain regional benefits likely accompanied that type of response. It is more difficult, however, to imagine the potential benefits associated with the other popular response: 'Betting on the Basics.' In other words, we are left wondering what (if any) are the benefits of 'Betting on the Basics'. Though the response as a whole was generally associated with lower adaptive resilience, the approach could not have been completely without merit. The Detroit case study provided ample evidence of potentially resilient outcomes in a region where the over-arching approach was still 'Betting on the Basics.' Markusen and Carlson (1988) also predicted potential benefits associated with the retention-oriented 'Betting on the Basics' approach. So, even though the response type was not generally associated with adaptive resilience, certain elements of this approach were likely still effective for regions adapting to deindustrialization. Knowing more about what worked and what did not would be useful to regions confronting similar challenges in the future.

Perhaps the most important remaining question is how useful these findings really are. In other words, what are the implications of this research for future economic development responses to slow-burning challenges? Though we cannot guarantee that every practitioner and policymaker will find these conclusions useful for their own regional challenges, there are certain elements of this research that will likely be helpful to anyone thinking about economic development responses to slow-burning challenges in the future. For instance, it may prove useful to know that, when faced with a slow-moving challenge like deindustrialization, most regional leaders will take steps to better position their region moving forward. Also key is that regions that respond quickly and incorporate a diverse group of stakeholders are likely to be better positioned to deal with such challenges.

In the end, we saw that the degree to which a regional economy was rooted in manufacturing likely played an important role in how much response and recovery resilience was exhibited in that region. Manufacturing, therefore, has a rather strong legacy, one that is often difficult to escape from. Still, some regions were able to move beyond their manufacturing legacy, and from their responses emerged another set of important lessons. In Chapters 5 and 6, we saw that regional responses of a more creative variety are more likely to be associated with adaptive resilience than are responses that focus solely on recreating the past. In terms of timing, swift responses were generally more likely to be associated with adaptive resilience than were slower responses.

Together, these findings suggest that we have indeed increased our understanding of how Rust Belt regions responded to the challenges of deindustrialization. More specifically, we find that the typologies designed by both Markusen and Carlson (1988) and Clavel and Kleniewski (1990) are quite useful in helping us to better understand regional responses to deindustrialization. Though numerous questions about causation remain, the typologies prove to be extremely useful for studies of economic development responses in regions experiencing economic restructuring. Findings from this study indicate that there was no one uniform response to deindustrialization across Rust Belt regions. Regions varied greatly in terms of the choices they made and the paths that they followed. As a result, some regions fared better than others, and some still search for the higher road. This study has helped us to identify commonalities across cases and group regions based upon the type of response they employed. Doing so brings us one step closer to understanding how regions might successfully respond to other economic challenges, including the Great Recession.

In light of the Great Recession

The Great Recession, which officially began in December 2007 and ended in June 2009, was a significant blow to the United States economy on the whole (NBER 2013). Across the US, however, regions experienced this downturn in myriad ways, leaving some regions stumbling and others relatively unscathed. For scholars interested in the concept of adaptive resilience, and especially for those with an interest in the Rust Belt, the Great Recession again offered a chance to think more about how and why regions vary in their ability to withstand and recover from economic shocks. In particular, it reignited the conversation about Rust Belt regions and their economic position within the broader United States economy (Stodola 2011; Tweh and Benman 2012; Weissmann 2012). In order to understand the performance of Rust Belt regions during and after the Great Recession, it is important to understand how they fared in the decade leading up to it.

Much like the rest of the United States, Rust Belt regions have experienced both highs and lows since the 1980s. As economic restructuring continued into the 2000s, most metropolitan Rust Belt regions experienced pronounced challenges, including continued population and job losses. While the Sunbelt dealt with rapidly growing economies and populations, most Rust Belt regions continued to bleed out, though the pace of the outmigration would hasten in most places over time. Some scholars have argued that this precipitous decline *before the Great Recession* helped many of these regions to buffer against the ill-effects that the rest of the United States began to feel at the end of 2007 (Friedhoff et al. 2012).

Prior suffering notwithstanding, what else made Rust Belt metros uniquely prepared for the Great Recession? Quite obviously, it was a combination of many factors. Much of it, either indirectly or directly, was related to the Rust

Belt's lack of a housing bubble. Over the last few decades, housing appreciation in most Rust Belt regions had been minor. So, while many other areas of the United States saw housing values appreciate to unsustainable levels leading into the fourth quarter of 2007, the Rust Belt had no such problem and therefore largely remained bubble-less and bust-less (Hexter and Coulton 2010). The National Association of Realtors noted that between 2006 and 2010, while the nation on the whole saw a decrease in median housing prices, the median increased by 22 percent in Buffalo, 5 percent in Pittsburgh, and 3.6 percent in Indianapolis (NAR 2014). In some ways, the stable housing markets in these regions acted as a 'remember function' for the regional economies as they adapted to the stresses seen in the national economy.

While other regions of the United States were sent into a tailspin, many Rust Belt regions became increasingly attractive as places to live and work, especially to college-educated young adults. William Frey of Brookings described how places like Pittsburgh and Columbus saw a net increase in college-educated adults between 2007 and 2009, and others, like Buffalo and Cleveland, achieved stability during that time period (Frey 2011). Richard Florida also observed these phenomena, so much so that he was moved to write that some older Rust Belt regions are "back on the talent map" (Florida 2011).

Reversing the brain drain and nurturing a stable housing market are goals that are directly in line with emerging economic development strategies observed in many of these regions. In addition to housing and workforce development strategies, Rust Belt regions have been actively cultivating their healthcare and educational institutions. Such an approach, commonly referred to as an 'Eds and Meds' strategy, has helped foster a more diverse economic base. Among the case study regions, Pittsburgh is often touted as a place that has navigated this change fairly well (Kaffer 2010; Detrick 1999). Its economic base looks radically different than it did in the 1970s and 1980s, thanks in part to investments by Carnegie Mellon University, University of Pittsburgh, and the University of Pittsburgh Medical Center, among others. However, scholars have warned about the potential risks involved, should every region pursue this approach (Cowell et al. *forthcoming*). Although it is not yet known whether choosing 'Eds and Meds' will set some places up for failure, due to oversaturation of certain sectors at the national scale, there are certainly reasons for concern. Not every region can have a biomedical or educational cluster strong enough to anchor the local economy, but if leaders in each place talk about how their region is well situated to do so, then it is hard to distinguish where it truly is a promising idea. Going forward, regional leaders would be wise to consider all of the alternatives and identify what other regions are pursuing as part of their own economic development strategies.

While the rise of 'Eds and Meds' is often linked to a corresponding decrease in manufacturing, Rust Belt regions have shown that this is not necessarily the case. Manufacturing still plays a key role in most of the regional economies of the case study regions and across the broader United States. Politicians and academics have loudly argued that we are on the verge of a *manufacturing moment,* as manufacturing in the US and other developed nations is poised to regain at least some of its competitive position. Researchers at the Boston Consulting Group and the National League of Cities predict that sectors like transportation goods, computers and electronics, fabricated metals, machinery, plastics, and rubber have reached a tipping-point and they expect to see increased production in the United States over the next decade (Helper et al. 2012; McFarland and McConnell 2011). Returning companies are beginning to 'reshore' because of growing concerns with quality, workforce competency, efficiency, speed to market, and supply chain vulnerabilities abroad. In the United States, manufacturing employment has increased 4.4 percent since a recent low of 1.14 million jobs in January 2010 (U.S. BLS 2013a). The Boston Consulting Group predicts that manufacturing growth could create between 2 million and 3 million jobs in the next decade with, an estimated 600,000 to 1 million of them being direct manufacturing jobs (Sirkin et al. 2012, 12). Though not all of these jobs will find their way to the Rust Belt, we can expect to see some positive effects in places like Detroit and Cleveland. Their reliance on auto and auto-parts manufacturing, two sectors that are experiencing particularly strong recoveries, should serve them well (Wial 2013). Again, the historical strengths and institutional memories related to automobile manufacturing in these regions may afford them a useful 'remember function' as they adapt to ongoing changes in the broader economy.

Unemployment within many Rust Belt regions has also been better than the national average throughout much of the post-Great Recession period. All but Cleveland and Detroit remain at or below 6.5 percent, which is the national average (U.S. BLS 2013b). Current-dollar Gross Metropolitan Product growth in many of the case study regions – namely, Cincinnati, Columbus, Detroit, Indianapolis, and Pittsburgh – also bested the national average in the post-recession period (U.S. BEA 2013). Similar trends can be seen in job growth figures for Rust Belt regions. According to Brookings' Metro Monitor, Buffalo, Columbus, Indianapolis, and Pittsburgh have all fared comparatively well in terms of job recovery since the Great Recession (Brookings 2014).

Even in the face of these optimistic developments, we are reminded that the Rust Belt remains a challenged place. Pervasive segregation, concentrated poverty, and fiscal insolvency plague many parts of the Rust Belt. The painful process of transitioning from heavy industry to a service sector-based economy continues today, many decades after it began. This has been especially true in the case of Detroit, which has become the preeminent focus of post-industrial scholarship. As such, a light has been shined on the city and region by a variety of scholars spanning the fields of architecture, economics, public health, sociology, and urban planning. What has been most fascinating about this scholarly scrutiny is how little consensus there is among scholars and practitioners about the current state and future of Detroit. The Detroit region remains a mesmerizing paradox. It is home to the 'Big Three,' vibrant arts and culture, a revitalizing urban core, innovative micro-solutions to vacancy and abandonment, and astonishingly wealthy suburban communities. At the same time, it is also home to widespread poverty and neglect, high unemployment, and fiscal insolvency, and is plagued by lingering issues related to General Motors and Chrysler, which experienced government-sponsored bankruptcy in 2008.

Scholars and practitioners are right to be concerned about how these conflicting messages impact those who live in the region and how the relentless push-pull of popular media and popular perception will affect the region in the long run. Scholars of resilience would be wise to take notice and continue to address the long-term and very public challenges playing out in Detroit and other Rust Belt metropolitan areas.

In the end, all this reminds us that there is still much work to do. On the final day of the 2013 Bruner Loeb Forum on Legacy City Design in Detroit, Professor Bob Shibley, Dean of the School of Architecture and Planning at University at Buffalo, issued a call to arms for practitioners and scholars in the audience. He ended his talk on the unique challenges and opportunities within Rust Belt cities by saying that, "You are not obligated to complete the work, but neither are you free to abandon it." Whatever the difficulties, these are words to truly live by.

References

Brookings. 2014. Metro Monitor. Accessed March 3, 2014. http://www.brookings.edu/research/interactives/metromonitor#/M10420.

Clavel, Pierre, and Nancy Kleniewski. 1990. "Space for Progressive Local Policy: Examples from the U.S. and the U.K." In *Beyond the City Limits*, edited by John Logan and Todd Swanstrom, 199–236. Philadelphia, PA: Temple University Press.

Cowell, Margaret, Juliet Gainsborough, and Kate Lowe. (forthcoming). "Adaptive Resilience and Mimetic Behavior: Economic Visions in the Great Recession." *Journal or Urban Affairs*.

Detrick, S. 1999. "The Post Industrial Revitalization of Pittsburgh: Myths and Evidence." *Community Development Journal* 34(1): 4–12.

Florida, Richard. 2011. "Where the Brains Are Going." *The Atlantic*. Accessed March 21, 2014. http://www.theatlantic.com/business/archive/2011/01/where-the-brains-are-going/69729/#.

Frey, William. 2011. "Migration Declines Further: Stalling Brain Gains and Ambitions." *State of Metropolitan America* 24. Accessed March 19, 2014. http://www.brookings.edu/research/opinions/2011/01/12-migration-frey.

Friedhoff, A., S. Kulkarni, and A. Berube. 2012. "Metro Monitor – December 2012." The Brookings Institution. Accessed March 2014. http://www.brookings.edu/research/interactives/metromonitor#US-recovery-overall-nv.

Helper, Susan, Timothy Krueger, and Howard Wial. 2012. *Why Does Manufacturing Matter? Which Manufacturing Matters? A Policy Framework*. Washington, DC: Brookings Metropolitan Policy Program.

Hexter, Kathryn Wertheim, and Claudia J. Coulton. 2010. "HUD's Regional Housing Scorecard Spotlights." *PD&R EDGE*, Online Magazine. Accessed March 15, 2014. http://www.huduser.org/portal/pdredge/pdr_edge_featd_article_022312.html.

Kaffer, Nancy. 2010. "Pittsburgh Faced Problems Much Like Detroit's – and Overcame Them, Leaders Say." *Crain's Detroit Business*. Accessed March 10, 2014. http://www.crainsdetroit.com/article/20100603/FREE/100609939/pittsburgh-faced-problems-much-like-detroits-and-overcame#.

Markusen, Ann, and Virginia Carlson. 1988. "Bowing Out, Bidding Down, and Betting on the Basics: Midwestern Responses to Deindustrialization in the 1980s." Center for Urban Affairs and Policy Research, Working Paper, Northeastern University, Boston, MA.

McFarland, Christiana K., and J. Katie McConnell. 2011. *Strategies for Globally Competitive Cities: Local Roles in Foreign Direct Investment*. Washington, DC: National League of Cities. Center for Research and Innovation.

National Association of Realtors (NAR). 2014. National Association of REALTORS® Median Sales Price of Existing Single-Family Homes for Metropolitan Areas.

National Bureau of Economic Research (NBER). 2013. US Business Cycle Expansions and Contractions. Accessed May 16, 2013. http://www.nber.org/cycles.html.

Sirkin, Harold L., Michael Zinser, Douglas Hohner, and Justin Rose. 2012. "U.S. Manufacturing Nears the Tipping Point: Which Industries, Why, and How Much?" Chicago, IL: Boston Consulting Group.

Stodola, Sarah. 2011. "Rust Belt Revival? Thank the Recession." *The Fiscal Times*. November 17, 2011.

Tweh, Bowdeya, and Keith Benman. 2012. "Three Years After the Great Recession: Legacy Dims Hope to Break Economic Malaise." NWITimes. June 24, 2012. Accessed May 15, 2014. http://www.nwitimes.com/business/local/three-years-after-the-great-recession-legacy-dims-hope-to/article_ee0ed8a4-e75c-54c6-bedc-68b902cbcb72.html.

U.S. Bureau of Economic Analysis (BEA). 2013. GDP by Metropolitan Area. Regional Economic Accounts.

U.S. Bureau of Labor Statistics (BLS). 2013a. Current Employment Statistics. Employment, Hours, and Earnings from the Current Employment Statistics Survey.

U.S. Bureau of Labor Statistics (BLS). 2013b. Local Area Unemployment Statistics. Unemployment Rates for Metropolitan Areas.

Weissmann, Jordan. 2012. "The Revenge of the Rust Belt: How the Midwest Got its Groove Back." *The Atlantic*. Accessed March 1, 2014. http://www.theatlantic.com/business/archive/2012/05/the-revenge-of-the-rust-belt-how-the-midwest-got-its-groove-back/257541/.

Wial, Howard. 2013. "Metropolitan Economies in the Great Recession and After." Prepared for presentation at the Allied Social Science Associations/Labor and Employment Relations Association annual meetings, San Diego, January 4, 2013. Accessed March 27, 2014. http://www.google.com/url?sa=t&rct=j&q=&esrc=s&source=web&cd=1&cad=rja&uact=8&ved=0CCcQFjAA&url=http%3A%2F%2Fwww.uic.edu%2Fcuppa%2Fcued%2FMetropolitan_Economies_in_the_Great_Recession_and_After.docx&ei=L0krU_71JYSs2wW-vICAAg&usg=AFQjCNFncwF9zFRX1kFboADHW3oh1IHHWA&sig2=wQOPKGeiSY4E8dAXJsSQ3g&bvm=bv.62922401,d.b2I.

Index

For Product Safety Concerns and Information please contact our EU representative GPSR@taylorandfrancis.com Taylor & Francis Verlag GmbH, Kaufingerstraße 24, 80331 München, Germany